The Great War

– ORIGINS, NATURE & AFTERMATH –

Ronald Cameron

(Principal Teacher of History, Tain Royal Academy)

Pulse Publications

CONTENTS

Note about the war artists

The paintings reproduced in this book were painted by artists with first-hand experience of the war. Paul Nash and John Nash served in the Artists Rifles before they were appointed as official war artists. Sir William Orpen became an official war artist after serving in the army service corps. CRW Nevinson served in the Royal Army Medical Corps. His painting, 'Paths of Glory', was suppressed by the government at the time as it depicted dead soldiers. John Singer Sargent was an American eyewitness of the war who was appointed as an official was artist by the British government.

ACKNOWLEDGEMENTS

The author and pubisher would like to thank the following for permission to reproduce copyright material.

The Imperial War Museum for photographs and paintings on pages 5, 6, 16, 17, 18, 19, 20, 21, 22, 23, 25, 27, 28, 31, 32, 33, 35, 37, 38, 40, 42, 43, 46, 47, 50, 51, 52, 53, 54, 55, 56, 57, 59, 62, 67, 71 and the front cover; The Illustrated London News for photographs on pages 8, 10, 44, 72; Punch for cartoons on pages 15, 76, 78; The Tate Gallery for the painting on page 19; Sächsische Landesbibliothek for the painting on page 69 and the detail on the back cover.

Sketches on pages 24, 26 and 50 are by Fiona MacGregor.

The Front cover is a painting by Georges Leroux called *L'Enfer*.

Published and typeset by
Pulse Publications
45 Raith Road, Fenwick,
Ayrshire, KA3 6DB

Printed and bound by
J Thomson Colour Printers

British Library Cataloguing-in-Publication Data

A Catalogue record for this book is available from the British Library

ISBN 0 948 766 67 0

© Cameron 1999

1 The Origins of the Great War

While they were fighting the First World War the people of Europe were, on the whole, confident that they knew why they were fighting. The French, Belgians and Russians were fighting to defend their homeland from an aggressive enemy. The British were fighting to prevent Europe being dominated by arrogant, aggressive Germany and to save gallant little Belgium from being devoured by that very state. The Germans, on the other hand, believed their Kaiser (Emperor) when he argued that they were taking pre-emptive action—striking first—to save the Fatherland from destruction by enemies massing to both the east and the west.

When the war was over and nine million soldiers lay dead, Europeans looked again at the causes of the conflict and realised that they were no longer certain why it had happened. The debate continues. Although it is impossible to provide an explanation of the war which will receive general agreement, one can piece together the broad outlines of the events leading up to it and review some of the arguments that surround these events.

What, then, led to the outbreak of general European war in August 1914?

The Franco-Prussian war of 1870

There is a tendency for each war to have its origins in the previous one. At the start of the 19th century, Germany was not one country but a collection of small kingdoms and principalities under the influence of Austria. Gradually the Kingdom of Prussia (not to be confused with Russia), which was centred round Berlin, grew to challenge Austria's authority.

In 1866 Austria itself was defeated by Prussia in a short and nasty war. Then in 1870 Otto von Bismarck, the Prussian Chancellor, tricked the French into declaring war on Prussia. The smaller German states rallied to Prussia and the French army was destroyed in a seven week war. Napoleon III, the French Emperor, was captured and Paris fell, after a long siege which reduced the city to starvation.

The French were forced to sign a peace treaty in the old Royal Palace of Versailles, a few miles out of Paris. They had to pay a large indemnity (fine) and lost the key border provinces of Alsace and Lorraine to the new German Empire which was proclaimed with the King of Prussia as its Kaiser. France never accepted the loss of these territories. They were rich in iron and coal and, although of mixed population, most of the people wanted to be part of France.

THE GROWTH OF POWER BLOCKS
The Central Powers

To gain revenge France needed allies. Consequently, Bismarck tried to make treaties with every significant European state to prevent France from doing so.

The Dual Alliance 1879

Forgetting the war of 1866, Germany and Austria-Hungary agreed to help each other if either were attacked by a third force. Austria and Russia were rivals for control of the small states of southeast Europe called the Balkans and Germany feared France.

The Triple Alliance 1882

When France and the newly united state of Italy fell out over trade, Bismarck seized his chance and offered Italy a defensive treaty. This created a power block in Central Europe called the Triple Alliance or Central Powers. Italy, however, would never be a reliable member. She had only recently won her freedom from Austrian influence and wanted border provinces which were still under Austrian rule. As the First World War approached it was said that Italy would rush to the aid of the winner.

The Allies – France Finds Friends

By 1907 a second power block, known as 'the Allies' to the British, had emerged. It consisted of France, Russia and Britain,

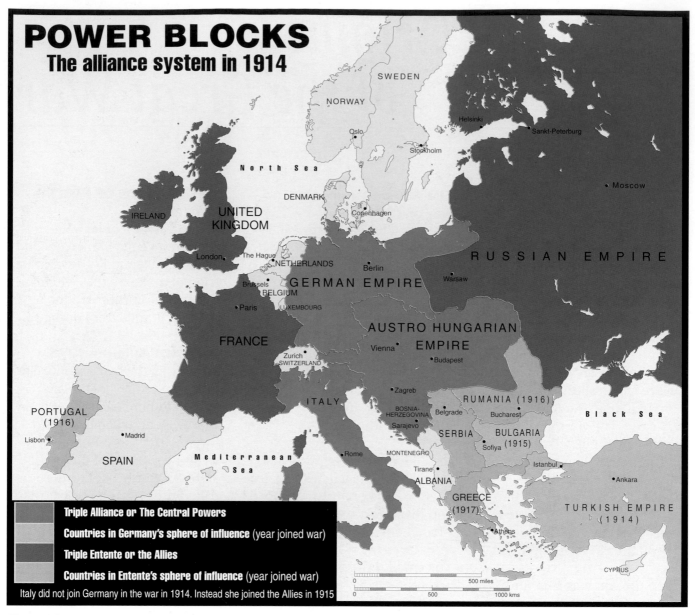

POWER BLOCKS
The alliance system in 1914

Triple Alliance or The Central Powers

Countries in Germany's sphere of influence (year joined war)

Triple Entente or the Allies

Countries in Entente's sphere of influence (year joined war)

Italy did not join Germany in the war in 1914. Instead she joined the Allies in 1915

Figure 1.1

three countries whose traditional dislike of each other was only exceeded by their fear of Germany.

1894 Franco-Russian Alliance

In 1888 Germany got a new Kaiser, Wilhelm II, who sacked Bismarck and gave up trying to stay on good terms with both Russia and Austria-Hungary. France stepped in with the offer of a defensive alliance. Russia signed and the Triple Alliance found itself facing potential enemies to east and west and having to divide its forces to fight a war on two fronts. Russia was a very backward and primitive state but it was beginning to in-

dustrialise and with a population of over 125 million had huge military potential.

Britain Joins in

At the end of the 19th century Britain followed a policy of 'splendid isolation'. Her main concern was with her huge, globe-spanning Empire. She did not see herself as a European power and therefore had a comparatively small land army which would be capable of fighting in Europe. She had the world's biggest navy to defend the trade of her far-flung Empire. Britain's democratic politicians disliked the autocratic government of Russia where the

Czar had absolute and undisputed power. A Russian invasion of India, the jewel in the crown of the British Empire, through Afghanistan, was also feared. Eight hundred years of almost constant warfare and intense rivalry over their Empires characterised Britain's relationship with France. These were two nations with an intense distrust and dislike of each other. Of all the nations of Europe, Britain felt closest to Germany, whose new Kaiser was the Grandson of Queen Victoria. In driving Britain into an alliance with France the new Kaiser had achieved the near impossible. How did he manage it?

In 1897 Germany began a programme to expand its navy considerably. Since Britain could only be attacked from the sea this was seen as threatening. Furthermore, the Kaiser openly sided with the Boers, South African farmers of Dutch origin, in their struggle to remain independent from Britain. Britain felt very isolated during the Boer War (1899–1901) as she finally crushed Boer freedom in defiance of European condemnation of her 'bully boy' tactics.

The Anglo-Japanese Alliance 1902

Since there was nobody in Europe who would have anything to do with her, Britain turned to the new, emerging industrial power of Japan for support. This alliance enabled Britain to withdraw some of her naval strength from the Pacific and to concentrate it in Europe. In 1904, however, war broke out between Russia and Japan when Russia appeared to challenge Japan's control of Korea. Neither Britain nor France wanted to be dragged into this war and fight each other on behalf of their allies so they were obliged to speak to each other and agreed to stay out.

1904 The Entente Cordiale (Anglo-French Agreement)

The discussions over the Russo-Japanese war rapidly moved on to other topics. Numerous disputes over colonies were settled and the mutual fear of Germany was discussed. The agreement which resulted, the Entente Cordiale (friendly agreement) stopped short of a full formal alliance. Britain did not promise to go to war if France was attacked, but vague assurances were given that it was not in Britain's interest for France to be conquered by Germany.

The Anglo-Russian Entente 1907

Britain reached a similar, informal agreement with Russia in 1907 completing the division of Europe into two rival power blocks, each very suspicious of the other. Various other factors were also in play by this stage to crank up the tension between them.

CRANKING UP THE TENSION – OTHER FACTORS LEADING TO WAR

Factor 1 The Arms Race

Table 1.1 shows clearly that Europe was an uneasy place in the years before the war.

The countries of mainland, continental Europe competed with each other to build up both the size of their armies and the levels of equipment they possessed. This was partly driven by fear of what might happen if they fell behind their rivals. Germany chose to compete in two arms races, a military one with her continental rivals and a naval one with Britain. In 1903 von Bethmann Hollweg, later Chancellor of Germany said:

"The first and basic idea (of the Kaiser) is to smash the global position of Britain in favour of Germany. It is for this reason, so the Kaiser is firmly convinced, that we need a navy ..." (quoted by Fritz Fischer in *From Kaiserreich to Third Reich*)

In 1897 Germany decided to create a fleet of nineteen battleships, twelve heavy cruisers and thirty light cruisers. These numbers were doubled in 1906. This was not enough to threaten Britain which, at that time, operated to the two power standard—the Royal Navy was always as strong as the next two most powerful fleets combined. Britain, nevertheless, responded by building ships and a fierce naval arms race ensued. In 1906 the HMS Dreadnought was launched, the fastest, most powerful and most heavily armoured battleship afloat. No other ship could stand against it and at a stroke it made every other battleship in the world obsolete (out of date). Since Dreadnoughts were now the ships that mattered, Germany could more easily catch up on Britain's lead by simply building Dreadnoughts.

(continued on page 8)

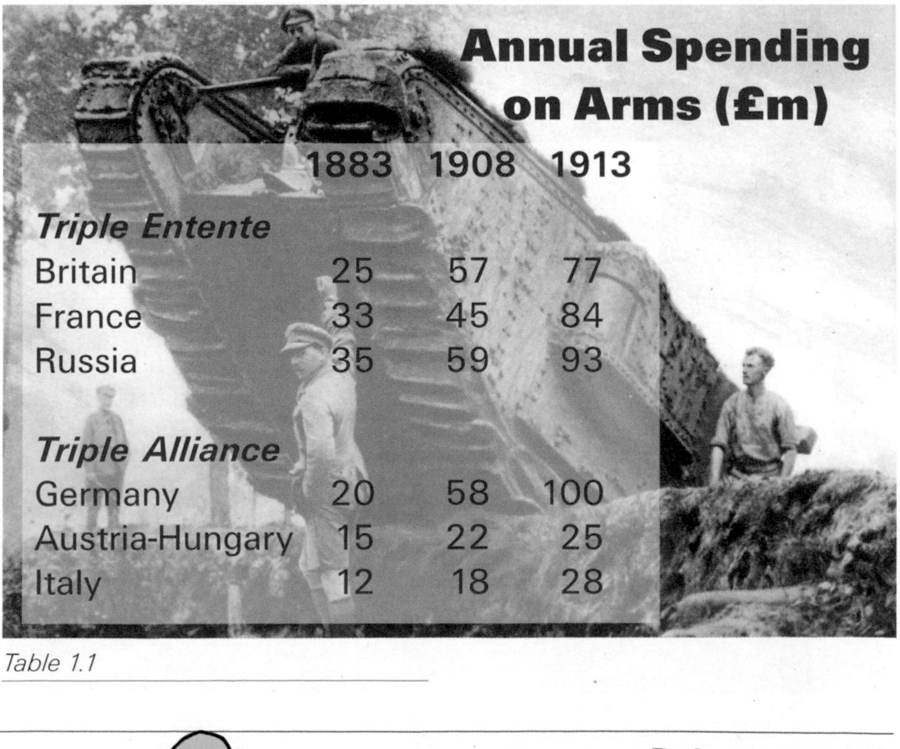

Annual Spending on Arms (£m)			
	1883	1908	1913
Triple Entente			
Britain	25	57	77
France	33	45	84
Russia	35	59	93
Triple Alliance			
Germany	20	58	100
Austria-Hungary	15	22	25
Italy	12	18	28

Table 1.1

DREADNOUGHT

At the time of the Battle of Trafalgar (1805) the Royal Navy was equipped with wooden-hulled sailing ships with muzzle-loading canons protruding from openings in their sides. In the course of the 19th century sail gave way to steam, wooden walls were replaced by steel armour plate and canons by breach-loading guns. Nelson fought the French at Trafalgar side by side, line abreast at point-blank range because his canons had a very limited range of about a mile. The new naval guns were much more powerful. At Jutland in 1916 the British and German fleets engaged at a range of 16,000 yards (9.1 miles / 14.5km).

Before Dreadnought, iron clad battleships usually had a mixture of gun sizes. These were mounted on the sides of the ship and were sometimes so close to the waterline that they could not be fired in heavy seas. Dreadnought had ten huge 12 inch guns which were mounted mainly in rotating steel turrets on the fore and aft decks. These guns had a 12 inch bore (barrel diameter), fired shells weighing almost one ton and could be brought to bear on targets on either side of the ship. Those on older ships could only cover targets on one side. Photographs of Dreadnought show that four of her ten guns were mounted amidships, a feature which was eliminated from later Dreadnoughts and 'super-Dreadnoughts'.

Dreadnought's gunfire was also centrally controlled from the 'spotting top', halfway up her mast. Giant optical range finders were used to calculate the range and direction of targets before this information was telephoned to the gun crews. Firing salvos of shells at extreme range, the guns would be angled upwards at about 33 degrees and the shells would fall on their target from many thousands of feet.

Dreadnought's steam turbine engine gave her a speed of 21 knots, 3 or 4 knots faster than any other comparable ship. Thus no big ship could stand against her and only the smaller warships were fast enough to run away. She quickly became obsolete herself and spent most of the war with a squadron of pre-Dreadnoughts defending the Thames estuary where she rammed and sank the German submarine U-9.

HMS Dreadnought (© Imperial War Museum)

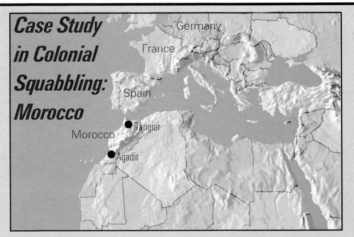

Empire of:	Area(Km^2)	Population
Britain	33,000,000	400,000,000
France	11,500,000	56,000,000
Germany	2,950,000	12,000,000
Belgium	2,400,000	15,500,000
Holland	2,000,000	38,000,000
Japan	300,000	17,000,000

Table 1.2 Source Quoted in Passant A short history of Germany

Colonial Empires in 1914

1905 The First Moroccan Crisis

The French had been trying for a number of years, with limited success, to conquer Morocco. The Kaiser arrived at the port of Tangiers in his Royal yacht and delighted the Moroccans by pledging Germany's support for their independence under their Sultan. The French were less than pleased and war seemed a distinct possibility. Some thought the Germans were making a play for Morocco as part of their own empire, others that Wilhelm was merely showing off. He may have been testing the new entente between Britain and France in the hope that he could renew their age-old quarrels over Empire. After all, they had all but gone to war, as recently as 1898, over the Fashoda incident in the Sudan. If this was indeed the Kaiser's scheme it backfired badly on him. An international confer-

Case Study in Colonial Squabbling: Morocco

ence was called at Algeçeras in Spain. Britain proved that she could not even be relied on to justify her reputation for treachery and unreliability ('Perfidious Albion') and backed the French, as did the USA. The poor old Kaiser had got egg all over his face. France got Morocco and Wilhelm went home angry and humiliated.

1911 The Second Moroccan Crisis

Wilhelm II was not a man to learn by his mistakes. In 1911 the French were busy shooting Moroccans again, this time at the request of the Sultan, against whom they were revolting. The Kaiser protested that if the French were going to take over Morocco he should be given the French Congo as compensation. The German gunboat, SMS Panther, was dispatched to the Moroccan port of Agadir—in theory to protect German traders, in practice to put pressure on the French.

This latter action touched a raw nerve with the Brit-

ish who saw it as an attempt to establish a naval base opposite Gibraltar, from where they controlled access to the Mediterranean. Britain prepared for war. Again Wilhelm was forced to back down in the face of united opposition. Although he was given a strip of the French Congo as a sweetener he went off in the huff to build an even bigger navy. In 1912 Haldane, the British War Minister, went to Berlin to try and negotiate an end to the naval arms race. He failed. Britain then left the French Navy to control the Mediterranean while her fleet was withdrawn from Malta and Cyprus and sent to such sunny ports as Scapa Flow, Invergordon and Rosyth to face the Germans across the North Sea. The argument over Morocco, whatever its purpose, had led to a huge increase in tension.

Factor 2 Colonial Rivalry

In the last three decades of the 19th century, European nations divided most of Africa among themselves to give them colonies. Germany only entered this 'Scramble for Africa' in its final stages as she only became a unified country in 1870 and at first the Chancellor, Bismarck, was not interested in colonies. Because of this, Germany acquired only a small colonial empire in Africa, the Pacific and Asia.

A large colonial empire made a country look important and powerful. Colonies were seen as an important source of raw materials for the 'mother country's' industries and a market for her products. They provided Britain with places in which its surplus population could settle and they could also provide soldiers in wartime. This worked better in theory than in practice.

> "The colonies did not attract many German emigrants. Trade with them amounted to less than 1% of the German total. In 1914 they cost the German taxpayers in subsidies six times what the German merchants and investors made out of them in profits."
> (AJP Taylor, *The Course of German History* page151)

Wilhelm II is said to have been intensely jealous of the huge Empires of Britain and France. His attempts to secure Germany's rightful 'place in the sun' caused confrontations and crises, suspicion and ill-feeling. Colonial rivalry should be seen as a cause of increased tension rather than as a major cause of the war itself.

Factor 3 Trade Rivalry

Britain had been the world's first industrial power, but by the end of the 19th century she had been overtaken by Germany

Kaiser Wilhelm II became Kaiser in 1888. He despised democracy and was determined to be an old-fashioned style of King, ruling the country himself.

and the USA, especially in the newest hi-tech industries such as chemicals, electrical equipment, steel and motor vehicles. British businessmen found themselves being pushed out of markets in South America and Asia which they had regarded as theirs. It has been argued that this caused resentment which made Britain more willing to fight Germany. On the other hand, Britain and Germany had a substantial amount of trade with each other which would be ruined by war.

Factor 4 The Personality of the Kaiser

Wilhelm II became Kaiser in 1888. He despised democracy and was determined to be an old-fashioned style of King, ruling the country himself. By this time Germany had become one of the world's leading industrial powers and clearly needed a more modern style of government. Many middle-class Germans would have liked an elected Reichstag (parliament) to take over many of the royal powers.

Due to an accident at birth Wilhelm had a withered left

arm. As a child he had little contact with his parents who were always too busy being royal to spend time with him. As a young man he enjoyed the company of soldiers and became a good horseman and a good shot. Unfortunately, as we saw in the Moroccan crises, he was almost totally lacking in tact and offended people wherever he went, even when he did not intend to do so. He was happiest in the company of soldiers and usually took the advice of generals, or Admiral Tirpitz, rather than that of civilians. His Germany was very militaristic. This means that the armed forces had a lot of influence and that its leaders usually appeared in public in army uniforms. The army, in fact, dominated the country.

Many historians are reluctant to blame any one person, or country, for the war. They say that it was really just a huge accident which nobody wanted to happen. For instance, David Lloyd George, Britain's Chancellor of the Exchequer at the outbreak of war said:

> "Among the rulers and statesmen (of Europe) one can see now clearly that not one of them wanted war; certainly not on this scale. The possible exception is the foolish Berchtold, the Austrian Premier…. The last thing the vainglorious Kaiser wanted was a European war … Austrian and German rulers … had a hankering desire for a small war against a tiny neighbour who, standing alone, would speedily and easily be overwhelmed."
> (*War memoirs of David Lloyd George* page 34)

In 1961 Fritz Fischer, Professor of History at Hamburg University, caused a major storm in his country by arguing that the Kaiser went to war to strengthen his own position in Germany.

German industry and the German middle class had grown enormously. Educated townspeople and trades union leaders wanted a say in how the country was run. They wanted an elected Reichstag to run Germany. This was a threat to the Kaiser and the aristocrats (country landowners) who controlled Germany. Fischer argued that the Kaiser hoped a victory in war would make Germans more patriotic and loyal to him as King, forgetting their dreams of democracy.

> "For relations within Germany a grand passage of arms would not at all be a bad thing, even if it meant tears and pain for individual families."
> (*Armeeblatt*, an army magazine, in 1911. Quoted by Fischer in *From Kaiserreich to Third Reich* page 48)

THE BALKAN SITUATION

The alliance system linked together two areas of tension and instability in Europe. The first was in the west where France and Germany confronted each other over Alsace and Lorraine. The second was even more unstable, volatile and dangerous. In the southeast, Russia and Austria-Hungary were rivals for control of the Balkans. With the wisdom of hindsight we can see that a quarrel breaking out in either area could rapidly escalate into a European, or even global, war because of the alliances.

Southeastern Europe, or the Balkans had fallen under the control of the Ottoman Turks who advanced into Europe after 1400. In 1529 they besieged Vienna, the Austrian capital, but failed to capture it. Gradually, over the years, as the Ottoman Empire became weak and went into decline, the Turks were forced back. Much of the land fell under the control of the Hapsburg Empire. The Hapsburgs were the royal family of

German-speaking Austria. Other areas achieved their independence. The orthodox Christian Greeks, who had been ruled with great brutality by the Moslem Turks, regained their independence in 1821. Serbia won autonomy in 1830 and complete freedom in 1878, as did Bulgaria, a year after Rumania.

The Austrian Hapsburgs had pieced together a massive empire in which they ruled over, and looked down on, huge numbers of non-German peoples such as the Magyars of Hungary. Many of the others, such as the Poles, Czechs, Slovaks, Croats, Slovenes and Bosnian Serbs were Slavs. The Slavs are a racial group who speak very similar languages. The Serbs of the Hapsburg Empire began to look to the greatest Slav nation of all, Russia, for help and inspiration to break free from German domination. Later, independent Slav nations like Serbia and Bulgaria served as an example to them. An idea, called Pan-Slavism, emphasising Russia's historic mission to free all Slavs from Hapsburg or Ottoman rule, became popular in the Balkans.

As Slav nationalism grew, Austria feared its effects on her own subject peoples such as the Czechs. Russia sensed an opportunity to extend her influence in the Balkans.

Bosnia-Herzegovina: The Crisis of 1908

This area had been part of the Ottoman Empire and, for this reason, still has the largest Moslem population of any part of Europe, outside Turkey. In the 1870s its Serb people were keen to join newly independent Serbia. The Turks crushed their revolts with such cruelty that the great powers of Europe decided,

DEATH AT SARAJEVO

"On 28th June 1900 the Archduke Franz Ferdinand married Countess Sophie Chotek … It was a subdued, sad ceremony … Sophie Chotek was a mere countess; she did not come within the permitted degrees for an imperial Hapsburg marriage. …(she) did not become an archduchess or a royal highness.

Franz Ferdinand was a brutal and obstinate man, impatient with opposition, unsuited to a democratic age. He had one redeeming feature. He loved his wife. It irked him that she could never share his splendours, could never sit by his side on any public occasion. There was one loophole … His wife could enjoy the recognition of his rank when he was acting in a military capacity. Hence he decided … to inspect the army in Bosnia … the Archduke and his wife could ride in an open carriage side by side on 28th June—the anniversary of their wedding day. Thus for love did the Archduke go to his death …

When the Archduke's visit was announced, half a dozen … school boys decided to have a shot at him. They received encouragement and some crude weapons from a Serb secret

The Archduke Ferdinand and his wife just before the assassination.

society … One young conspirator failed to draw his revolver; another felt sorry for the Archduke's wife and went home; a third threw a bomb and missed. The Archduke reached the town hall. He was now angry: his wife's treat had been spoiled. He decided to drive straight out of town. But his chauffeur was not told. He took the wrong turning, then stopped the car and reversed. Gavrilo Princip saw before him, to his amazement, the stationary car. He stepped onto the running board; killed the Archduke with one shot … and hit (his) wife … with a second. She too died almost instantly. Such was the assassination at Sarajevo."

(AJP Taylor, *The First World War* pages 13-14)

Franz Ferdinand's last words were "Don't die Sophie, live for our children". It was too late. She was already dead.

The bomb thrower being taken into custody after the assassination.

at the Congress of Berlin in 1878, that Austria-Hungary should rule the area although it would officially still be part of the Ottoman Empire.

In 1908, faced with a rising tide of Serb nationalism, Austria-Hungary decided to annex the province (take it over completely). The Serbs were furious and Russia could do nothing to help them as she was still weak following her devastating defeat in the Russo-Japanese war of 1904–05. The Russians felt humiliated and were determined to do better next time. This is a dangerous state of mind in international affairs.

THE BALKAN WARS
First Balkan War: 1912
Encouraged by the Russians, Bulgaria, Serbia, Montenegro and Greece set upon and defeated Turkey with the intention of dividing up Macedonia, then still under Turkish rule.

Second Balkan War: 1913
The victors fell out among themselves while dividing the spoils. Bulgaria attacked Greece and Serbia and was in turn invaded by Turkey and Rumania! Bulgaria lost. She had to give land to Rumania. Greece and Serbia divided Macedonia between them as Bulgaria had feared. The European significance of these undignified little scuffles was threefold.

1 Turkey all but ceased to have any land in Europe.
2 The Bulgarians took the huff and fought for Germany to get their own back on Serbia in the First World War.
3 Serbia doubled in size and began to take a very cocky, 'in your face' attitude to Austria-Hungary over Bosnia.

Sarajevo: The Spark that lit the fire
By 1914 the European situation was so unstable that any tiny incident could start a war. This was most likely to happen in the Balkans and, indeed, it did in Sarajevo, Bosnia.

The Black Hand
Serb nationalists in Bosnia had established a secret society called the Black Hand whose aim was the union of their province to Serbia. They specialised in terrorist attacks on Austrian officials, such as judges, police and customs officers, with the aim of making the area too dangerous for Austrians to remain in. They received training and weapons from officers in the Serb army, but probably without the knowledge of the Serb government.

In a gesture calculated to be provocative, the Austrians sent the Archduke Franz Ferdinand, heir to the Hapsburg throne, and his wife, Sophie, on a state visit to Sarajevo, capital of Bosnia, on Sunday 28 June 1914. Over the border in Serbia they were celebrating Serbia's Independence Day. Franz Ferdinand was not a popular man in Austria.

> "(he) was one of the worst products of the Hapsburg House, reactionary, … brutal, and overbearing, he was also often insane. He lacked even the pessimism and hesitation which had made Francis Joseph a tolerable ruler."
> (AJP Taylor, *The Hapsburg Monarchy* page 242)

However, when he and Sophie were gunned down by the Black Hand, the Austrians could not resist the temptation to settle with dangerous Serbia, once and for all.

Serious rioting followed the assassination. Many Serbs living in Bosnia were executed. Princip could not be executed because he was under 21. He was sentenced to 20 years of hard labour but died in an Austrian gaol in April 1918, aged 23.

On 5 July, the Austrians sounded out their German allies and were assured of support if they took action against Serbia.

On 23 July, Austria-Hungary sent an ultimatum to Serbia. An ultimatum is a list of demands which must be met or a threat will be carried out. In this case the threat was war and the terms had to be accepted in two days. Serbia accepted most of the terms but rejected two because they would have effectively destroyed her independence. She refused to have Austrian officers in her army or Austrian Ministers in her government.

On 29 July, Austria-Hungary declared war on Serbia and began an artillery bombardment of its capital, Belgrade. Serbia appealed to Russia for help.

On 30 July, Russia began to mobilise her army—to prepare it for war. Germany began to mobilise her army for war with Russia. The Germans issued an ultimatum to the Russians, ordering them to stop mobilising. This was ignored.

On 1 August, Germany declared war on Russia and France began to mobilise. The Germans then told the French that if they did not end mobilisation and hand over the vital border forts of Verdun and Toul, war would ensue.

Germany had already decided to invade France through Belgium and the Netherlands, should war break out. Troops were moved up to the border. Britain had always been very sensitive about Belgium as it is a small country with seaports very close to Britain. British policy had always been that no major naval power should ever be allowed to control Belgium. Prussia, like Britain, had guaranteed Belgium's independence and neutrality in 1839. Britain warned Germany to stay out of Belgium.

The Belgians rejected German demands to be allowed to march through their country and demanded that Belgium's neutrality be respected. The Kaiser dismissed the 1839 treaty as "a scrap of paper". On 3 August he declared war on France.

On 4 August German armies invaded Belgium and ignored a British ultimatum to withdraw. Britain declared war. The Kaiser was not too impressed by this as the British Expeditionary Force, the army to be sent to drive him out of Belgium, consisted of a mere 100,000 men. The Kaiser could put 2,200,000 in the field.

At this point 376 million Europeans were at war and the conflict was rapidly expanding. A localised conflict in SE Europe had grown into a continental war because of the alliance system.

Source

THE CAUSES OF THE WAR

There are in the country (Germany) forces making for peace but they are unorganised and have no popular leaders … The bulk of the workmen, artisans and peasants … are peace loving by instinct.

Some want war because … they think it is inevitable. And, as far as Germany is concerned, the sooner the better … The aristocracy is military in character. War alone can prolong its prestige and support its family interest. This social class, with the King of Prussia as its supreme head, realises with dread the democratisation of Germany and the increasing power of the socialist party, and considers its own days numbered.

The higher bourgeoisie (upper middle class) is no less troubled than the aristocracy … (some) manufacturers declare that the difficulties between themselves and their workmen originate in France, the home of revolutionary ideas and freedom—without France industrial unrest would be unknown.

Lastly, there are manufacturers of guns and armour plate, big merchants who demand bigger markets, bankers who are speculating on the coming of the golden age and the next war indemnity—all these regard war as good business.

(From a report to the French Minister for Foreign Affairs from Diplomats in Germany. In *Diplomatic Correspondence Respecting the War* published by the French Government December 1914. Printed by HMSO.

The Origin of the Western Front

THE SCHLIEFFEN PLAN

Armies prefer not to fight wars for which they have not planned. All armies have contingency plans which can be followed in the event of conflicts with their country's most likely enemies. When the German army went to war in 1914 they were following plans drawn up by Count Alfred von Schlieffen in 1905. Schlieffen died in 1913 and never saw his plans put into practice.

In making up his plan Schlieffen made the following assumptions.

1   In the event of war Germany would have to fight on two fronts. War against France or Russia alone was not going to happen.

2   Russia's army was utterly inefficient and would take at least seven weeks to mobilise. The outright defeat and occupation of Russia was not possible because of the sheer size of the country, the ability of its people to endure unimaginable suffering and its vicious winters. An invasion of Russia in 1812 had all but destroyed the army of the great French Emperor, Napoleon. Thirty years after Schlieffen's death the Russian winter would do the same for Adolph Hitler's Nazi army.

3   The French had a large, well-armed, modern, efficient army. In the event of war they would follow their Plan XVII and attack Alsace and Lorraine as vigorously as possible. In 1870 Prussia had been able to beat the French in seven weeks.

4   France's frontiers with Germany were heavily fortified. Her frontiers with Belgium were scarcely defended at all.

5   Britain would probably stay neutral in the event of war, but should she join France she could safely be ignored since she had only a tiny army available to fight in Europe.

From these assumptions came the Schlieffen plan.

The Schlieffen Plan

Stage 1
Defend Alsace-Lorraine and the Russian frontier with the most token of forces.

Stage 2
Invade France from the north through neutral Belgium and the Netherlands. Here the land was flat and the frontiers unfortified. Sweep well to the west of Paris then turn east and finally north to get between the French capital and the French armies on the frontier. France would now be forced to capitulate. A detailed timetable was laid down to achieve this in seven weeks.

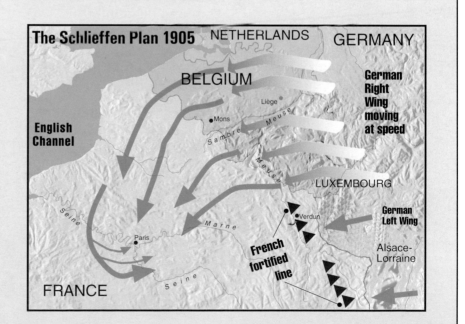

The Schlieffen Plan 1905

Stage 3
Transfer troops to the Eastern Front where the Russian bear would be emerging from hibernation. Gently persuade it to go back into its cave, but on no account follow.

Stage 4
Hold lavish victory celebrations.

THE PLAN IN PRACTICE

To begin with, the First World War was a war of movement, of rapid action and even cavalry charges. In the late summer of 1914 the German army had fought its way to within sight of the Eiffel Tower. It had taken them forty six days to get there but they failed to capture Paris or force the French to surrender.

In practice Schlieffen's plan did not quite work for the following reasons.

1   The Russian bear woke up too soon. Within ten days of the outbreak of war, two huge Russian armies had blundered into East Prussia, an area which is now part of Poland but which was part of Germany until 1944. Troops had to be diverted from the push on Paris. Outnumbered by more than two to one, the Germans smashed first one Russian army and then the other at the Battles of Tannenberg and the Masurian Lakes. The Russians lost perhaps 220,000 men—killed, wounded or captured. They also saved France.

2   The Germans diverted more troops to the defence of Alsace-Lorraine than Schlieffen had originally intended, again weakening the drive on Paris.

3   General Moltke, who led the German armies, decided not to invade Holland, only neutral Belgium. This caused severe congestion on the Belgian roads and slowed the Germans down .

4   The Belgians also slowed the Germans down by their stubborn defence of their concrete forts at Liège and Namur which lay in the German way.

5   The British got in the way. Before the war a British Expedi-

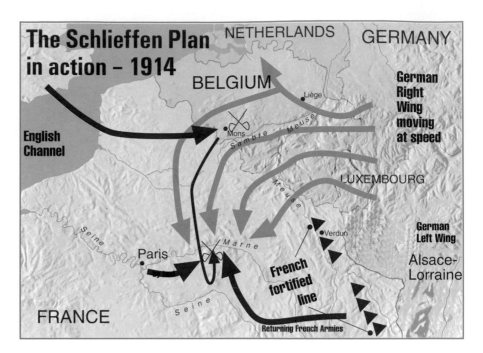

tionary Force (BEF) of about 100,000 men had been prepared for war in Europe. Although tiny by European standards, the BEF was a highly disciplined and trained professional force containing only volunteers and no conscripts. Equipped with the eight shot, short magazine Lee Enfield rifle, they took pride in their marksmanship and their ability to deliver fifteen rounds a minute. This halted the Germans, albeit briefly, at Mons in Southern Belgium.

"The Germans believed, and long after the war they went on believing, that the British had knocked them back with machine guns. But there were only two … and they made so conspicuous a target that they attracted the full force of the enemy fire. Team after team of gunners were knocked out. Time after time they were replaced, and on the canal bank the riflemen were firing … at a steady fifteen rounds a minute and they mowed down line af-

ter line of Germans."
(Lyn MacDonald, *1914* page 99)

A shortage of machine guns was one of the BEF's biggest problems. Retreating into France, another desperate rearguard action was fought at Le Cateau. When the BEF reached the River Marne near Paris they had marched and fought for 120 miles in twenty seven days. Their presence had helped to deflect the Germans from their course to the west of Paris and bounce them to the east into the path of the French army returning from Alsace.

6   German supply lines became overextended. Although struggling to keep up with their timetable, the Germans often got ahead of their supplies. Meticulous planning and the use of a highly efficient railway system could not deliver enough boots, bread, bandages, blankets, bullets etc. to the fast-moving troops. Like the British, they be-

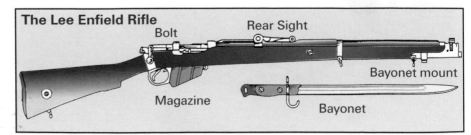

The Lee Enfield Rifle — Bolt, Rear Sight, Magazine, Bayonet mount, Bayonet

came exhausted. Inside their boots it was all blisters and no feet.

The First Battle of the Marne, September 1914

To the east of Paris, along the River Marne, the advancing Germans encountered three armies. In the centre was the remains of the BEF; to the east was the main French force, returning from the frontier; to the west were the garrison troops of Paris. Lacking transport, General Gallieni told his men to go out and hail taxis to take them to the battle front. The fare was as shown on the meter.

At this point new technology made its mark on the proceedings. The pilot of a British military aircraft noticed that the German force had split in two. The BEF began to advance into the gap. Fearing that his divided armies could be defeated in two battles, the German commander pulled his exhausted troops back, north of the Marne. Paris had been saved. The Schlieffen plan had failed.

The Race to the Sea

Once halted on the Marne, the Germans consolidated their position by digging trenches for their soldiers to shelter from enemy fire. The French dug trenches some distance from the German ones. The BEF left with all the speed they could muster and rushed off to secure the channel ports of Calais and Boulogne.

The Germans tried to outflank the French by going round on the west side. The French extended their trenches to the west. The Germans dug more trenches and tried another outflanking move. More French trenches frustrated their move. Soon the trench system reached the channel coast from where it extended 400 miles to the southeast and the border with Switzerland. The war of movement was at an end. The fighting would rage along this line of trenches for the next four bloody years with little movement in any direction.

The Christmas Truce, 1914

In October and November 1914 the Germans launched a fierce attack on the British-held city of Ypres (Ieper) in Belgium. They were repelled with heavy losses. Ypres was all but destroyed but became a symbol of defiance to which the British would cling stubbornly for the duration of the war. As Christmas approached it was clear that the war would not be over by then or, indeed, for a long time after that.

Christmas Day 1914 witnessed one of the most remarkable events of the conflict as British and German troops came out of their trenches and met in no-man's-land to share food, drink and tobacco, sing carols, bury their dead and play impromptu football matches. The truce did not take place all along the line. It did not happen in the French sectors. Usually it began with German troops from Saxony or Holstein who had little enthusiasm for the Prussian Kaiser's new Germany. Bavarian and Prussian troops rarely took part. The generals on both sides were most annoyed as they knew it would be hard for soldiers to start killing men with whom they had 'fraternised' the previous day. Orders were issued that it was not to happen again and most historians accept that the Christmas truce of 1914 was unique. Dennis Winter in *Death's Men: Soldiers of the Great War*, however, claims that events like it occurred here and there along the line every Christmas, especially where Saxons faced South of England Regiments.

BRAVO. BELGIUM!

The Technology of War

The First World War was a war fought from trenches. With the exception of East Africa, trenches appeared quickly wherever there was fighting. It did not just happen on the Western Front, but also on the Eastern Front, where the Russians fought the Austrians and the Germans, in Gallipoli and in Mesopotamia (now Iraq) where British Empire troops fought the Turks. Signs of this type of warfare had appeared during the American Civil War (1860–65) but there was very little of it during the Second World War (1939–45). This can be entirely explained by changes in weaponry and military technology. During the First World War the stage of development which weaponry had reached gave the advantage to the defending army. Defensive weapons were much more effective than attacking weapons. In a battle, casualties were usually much heavier on the attacking side. A man in a hole in the ground was much more likely to survive than one in the open. Most of the developments which led to this situation can be traced to advances in industry in the late 1800s.

MACHINE GUNS

Early guns could fire one bullet and then had to be reloaded. In the second half of the 19th century, rifles were developed with a small supply of bullets stored in a magazine. This greatly speeded up the reloading process. The standard British infantry rifle of the First World War, the Short Magazine Lee Enfield, had a magazine for eight bullets and, in the hands of a well-drilled soldier, could produce a rate of fire of fifteen rounds per minute. Infinitely more deadly than the rifle was the machine gun, a hideous weapon which

Vickers MG crew. Note the ammunition belt, coolant tube and early gas helmets. (© Imperial War Museum)

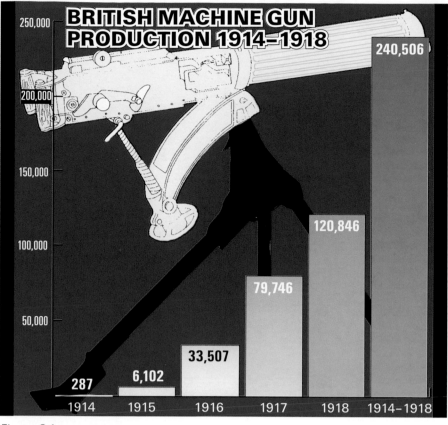

BRITISH MACHINE GUN PRODUCTION 1914–1918

Year	Production
1914	287
1915	6,102
1916	33,507
1917	79,746
1918	120,846
1914–1918	240,506

Figure 3.1

could fire up to 600 bullets per minute! The Gatling Gun, which appeared during the American Civil War, was the precursor of this type of weapon. Its multiple barrels rotated and fired with devastating effect as a gunner turned a handle. Mounted on cart wheels it was never going to be used in fast, mobile offensives.

In 1884 Hiram Stevens Maxim, an American inventor who had set up a workshop in London, designed a mechanism to eject the spent cartridge and load a fresh one using the recoil of the barrel. He also invented cordite, a smokeless propellant or gunpowder. His gun represented a huge advance and was used by the British to great effect in colonial wars in the late years of the 19th century against Africans armed mainly with spears. Lord Lugard helped himself to Uganda with two such weapons which were so temperamental that they could not be fired for

more than a few seconds before they overheated and jammed. The Ugandans did not know this and surrendered their kingdom after the briefest of demonstrations of the possibilities. A little rhyme from the time says

"Whatever happens we have got
the Maxim Gun and they have not."

Maxim cooperated with the British arms company, Vickers, to produce the Maxim-Vickers and the Vickers Mark 1, the standard British heavy machine gun of the First World War. Maxim's system was copied by every significant military power. British generals chose to ignore the obvious fact that other armies would have machine guns and at the start of the war the army had far too few of these weapons.

"Between August 1914 and June 1915 … contracts … were placed with Messrs. Vickers for … 1,792 machine guns. This would work out at two per battalion … The Germans were the only nation which had realised before the war the potentialities of the machine gun and they were arming their troops with 16 per battalion."
(*War Memoirs of David Lloyd George* pages 356 – 359)

Their supply was hugely increased and a special regiment, the Machine Gun Regiment, was set up to provide the infantry with machine gun support.

"The numbers we had in France at the date of the armistice were the equivalent of 80 per battalion."
(*War Memoirs of David Lloyd George* pages 360 – 364)

How the number of machine guns rose is shown in Figure 3.1.

Shrapnel from the shells killed many horses (© Imperial War Museum)

Sixty pounder gun in mud (© Imperial War Museum)

British forces had two standard machine guns, the Vickers and the Lewis, at this time. The Vickers Gun was a development on the earlier Maxim. .303 inch calibre bullets were fed through the weapon in a fabric belt. The barrel was surrounded by a water jacket, fed from a five gallon jerrycan. This was to keep the gun cool, but often after intense action the water would boil. Mounted on a tripod and manned by a team of three men, there was no way that anybody was going to run into action firing this 30kg beast. It was the defence or ambush weapon par excellence. Although very accurate and having a range of 4,100 metres, its gunners rarely aimed at specific targets. Against massed ranks of infantry they would turn the gun from one side to the other, spraying bullets almost as one would spray insects with an aerosol. This was a machine which could literally cut men in two or reduce their bodies to an unrecognisable pulp. To survive machine gun fire, trenches were essential.

The Lewis Gun was a lighter weapon invented by another American, Colonel Isaac Lewis. Gas pressure from the bullet fired was used to eject the spent cartridge and load the next bullet from a round pan magazine on top of the barrel. Like the Vickers and the Lee Enfield rifle it used standard .303 ammunition. Being air cooled it could not be fired for as long as the Vickers without overheating and jamming, but it was possible to carry it into attack even although the gunner had to lie down and support it on a bi-pod before firing. The Lewis was frequently mounted on British aircraft of this time.

The Machine Gun Regiment memorial in Hyde Park, Lon-

Howitzers in action (© Imperial War Museum)

Above: *Chateau Wood, October 1917. This shows the effects of shellfire on the land.* (© Imperial War Museum)

Below: *Void of War* by Paul Nash (©Tate Gallery)

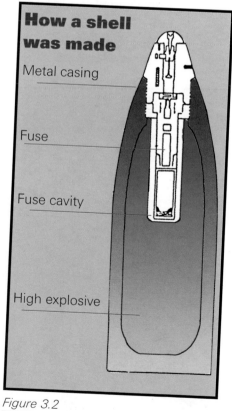

How a shell was made

Metal casing

Fuse

Fuse cavity

High explosive

Figure 3.2

don, bears the inscription "Saul has slain his thousands but David has slain his tens of thousands."

BARBED WIRE

Changes in iron and steel manufacturing in the late 19th century gave the technology to manufacture barbed wire which was used to strengthen trench defences by both sides. In places, the barbed wire entanglements in front of the German Hindenburg line on the Western Front were 20 metres wide. Soldiers emerged from their trenches at night to string the wire from steel pickets which screwed into the ground with a corkscrew action. Imagine trying to cross barbed wire while under rifle and machine gun fire. One method was to throw a corpse onto the wire and use it as a bridge.

ARTILLERY

Artillery are big, heavy guns which fire large projectiles designed to destroy buildings or fortifications or kill large numbers of soldiers. Artillery first appeared when gunpowder was brought to Europe in the 15th century. Muzzle loading cannons which fired a single round ball remained the order of the day until the second half of the 19th century when improving industrial technology revolutionised this form of weaponry. A hinged stopper, or breach, was fitted to the rear of the gun to do away with muzzle loading. The projectile, or shell, was also changed. It became conical, instead of round, was packed full of explosives, and was driven from the gun by an explosive charge in the shell case which remained in the breach after the shell had been fired. Late 19th century technology made it possible to cut a spiral groove

inside the barrel. This spun the shell and made it travel farther without being carried off course by wind. By 1914 the largest guns had a range of over 30 kilometres. Shells came in three sorts.

1 *High explosive:* These were designed to explode on impact and could wreck buildings. The blast, or explosive force, from such shells would also, of course, kill people.

2 *Shrapnel:* The shell was packed with round iron balls and fitted with a timer set to detonate it in the air over enemy lines. Lumps of red hot iron would then rain down on the unfortunates below, tearing some to pieces. George Coppard described the effect:

> "Jock Hershell left the dugout during shelling and didn't return … . I found him slumped in a heap, severely wounded …

Figure 3.3

Monthly production of shells for British 18pdr. field guns

	8,000,000
Autumn 1914	3,000
Spring 1915	400,000
Winter 1916	1,000,000
Winter 1917	8,000,000

Women were employed in factories to fill shells (© Imperial War Museum)

Trench mortar in use against the turks in the Middle East. Its rounds were affectionately known as plum puddings or toffee apples. (© Imperial War Museum)

Figure 3.3 shows the production of only one size of shell, by only one participating country. It was also a small shell at 18lbs (8.2kg). The largest weighed over 1 ton. French gunners could fire fifteen to twenty shells per minute from the famous '75' or 75mm gun, so huge numbers of these shells had to be made. At the end of the century, more than eighty years after the war, French and Belgian farmers still plough up their 'iron harvest' of over 500 tons of unexploded ordnance each year. Some of this is still live, very unstable and occasionally explodes causing injuries and death.

Trench mortars were a specialised form of artillery which added greatly to the casualty lists and to the misery of the men. Mortars were not a new weapon. Cumberland's redcoats had used early versions of them against the Jacobites at Culloden. In the 1980s and 1990s, homemade versions became popular weapons of terrorist organisations like the IRA. A short metal tube was used to fire steel drums packed with explosives and shrapnel (iron balls) high into the air so that they dropped straight down into the enemy trench. Soldiers could often see incoming mortar rounds which flew more slowly than standard artillery shells and often made a distinctive noise. Germans called trench mortars 'minenwerfer', meaning mine thrower. British Tommies called their shells 'moaning Minnies'.

At a glance I saw his broad back had caught a blast of shrapnel. I slit his tunic and underclothes with a jack-knife and separated them. I winced at the sight. Jock's back was full of punctures, and blood bubbles were wheezing out of holes as he breathed. Our hearts sank and we feared the worst. The backs of his powerful upper arms hung in shreds … It seemed like hours before we got him away to a first aid post, where we left him, knowing we would never see him again."
(George Coppard, *With a Machine Gun to Cambrai* pages 119–20)

3 Armour piercing: These specially hardened shells were designed to penetrate toughened steel before exploding. At the start of the war these were used mainly by the navy against warships but later they were used on land against tanks.

"It is part of the mythology of that war that the machine gun was the great killer of infantry. Actually, hospital statistics show that two-thirds of all wounds in all armies were caused by shells. It was gunfire which broke up the massed infantry attacks and it was largely

Gassed by John Singer Sargent *(© Imperial War Museum)*

Shelling produced the lunar landscapes associated with the First World War—demolished buildings, devastated forests, water-filled shell holes surrounded by mud. The constant noise of explosions and fear of a dreadful death unhinged men's minds. Shell shock is a form of nervous breakdown. A man might break after months or years at the front or after only hours of bombardment. Victims often shook uncontrollably, foamed at the mouth, wet themselves or just lay sobbing on the ground. Everyone has their breaking point. At first the British army regarded this as cowardice and shot some of the victims.

While artillery could kill entrenched soldiers, it was devastating against attackers in the open. In the Gulf War of 1991 it was estimated that a man in the open was two hundred times more likely to be killed by shelling than a man lying in a 50 cm deep ditch. First World War soldiers zig-zagged their trenches to limit the effects of blast and the Germans lined their dugouts with concrete.

CONCRETE

Improvements in cement manufacturing had made concrete a useful building material by 1900, when the Glenfinnan railway viaduct was built. During the First World War it was used, especially by the Germans, to build fortified machine gun posts or pill boxes and to strengthen the underground dugouts in which the men slept. The British and the French made less use of it. They hoped their lines would be temporary and that they could drive the enemy out of France. Concrete dugouts could resist all but direct hits from heavy artillery.

The overwhelming strength of defensive technology created a static war. Thousands of men died daily but nobody was going anywhere. It gave generals the problem of finding a method to break through the enemy line and get the war moving again. A number of new weapons were tried.

POISONOUS GAS

In the late 19th century Germany was the world leader in the chemical industry. In January 1915 the Germans used tear gas in an attack and then on 22 April 1915 they attacked with chlorine gas near Ypres. A memorial to the 3rd Canadian Brigade, which held their advance, stands on the spot at St Julien.

Chlorine gas is a nasty weapon. It was brought to the front in cylinders and released when there was a light wind to blow it towards the enemy line. It formed a green cloud and, being heavier than air, would quickly fill a trench. When breathed in it dissolved in the fluids of the lungs to form concentrated hydrochloric acid thus burning out the lungs.

"It produces a flooding of the lungs—the equivalent of drowning on dry land. The effects are these—splitting headache and terrific thirst (to drink water is instant death), a knife edge pain in the lungs and the coughing up of a greening froth … ending in insensibility and death. The colour of the skin from white turns a greenish black and yellow, the tongue

Indian troops display their gas masks (© Imperial War Museum)

protrudes and the eyes assume a glassy stare. It is a fiendish death to die."
(Malcolm Brown, *Tommy goes to War* published by JM Dent & Sons 1978)

Despite its fearsome effects gas never proved a decisive weapon. It needed light winds, but light winds can also be very variable and blow the gas back to its original owners. Contemporary accounts indicate that the British were especially adept at gassing themselves. Gas masks were quickly developed. Legend has it that the first was simply a handkerchief soaked in water and held to the nostrils. Water filters out chlorine. In dry weather soldiers were told to urinate on their handkerchiefs. Then came woollen flannel masks impregnated with chemi-

Horses and riders wore gas masks (© Imperial War Museum)

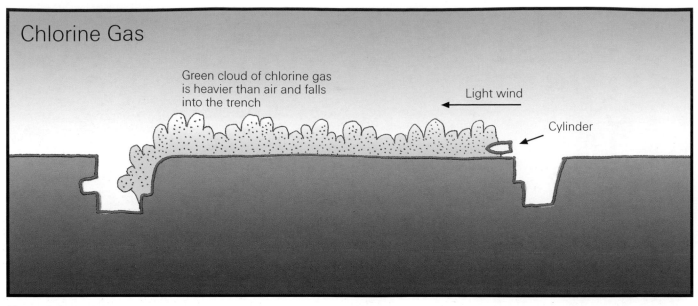

Figure 3.4

cals which irritated the skin and finally carbon filters connected by a tube to a rubber or canvas mask with glass eye pieces. These were hot and uncomfortable to wear but made survival possible.

All the new ideas on gas came from the Germans, with their advanced chemical industry. The use of chlorine was developed by a Jewish scientist called Fritz Haber. Then in December 1915 he went on to produce phosgene, a more powerful derivative of chlorine which was invisible. Next, in July 1917, he devised mustard gas, a liquid which looked like sherry and smelled of onions. It reacted vigorously when it came in contact with body fluids. It could burn out a man's lung and if a little got onto a sweaty part of the body it caused horrific burns and blisters. It brought about the end of the kilt as battle uniform in the British army. Towards the end of the war a group of Scottish soldiers crossed land which had been contaminated by the gas which went up their kilts and wreaked havoc in their groin areas. At the outset of the Second World War the War Office said that the kilt was not to be worn in battle. Mustard gas could be put into shells and fired behind the enemy lines if the wind was blowing in the wrong direction for a conventional attack. A special gas mask was needed to combat this menace.

Samples of Haber's gases were collected and analysed by the British Chemical weapons establishment at Porton Down and quickly copied. Haber also

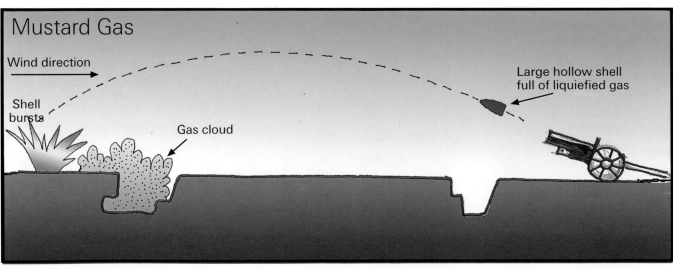

Figure 3.5

Tank going through the wire at Wailly training ground (© Imperial War Museum)

invented nerve gas, which was not used during the war, and Cyclon B which Hitler later used to murder millions of Haber's fellow Jews. Haber died in Switzerland in 1934, thus escaping this fate.

Because of the effectiveness of counter measures, gas proved to be an ineffective weapon. Although its victims died horrible deaths, with some dying coughing their lungs out years after the war, it did not kill enough soldiers to give either side a breakthrough. About 90,000 soldiers, out of the 9,000,000 who died on all sides, were accounted for by gas. Most of these were Russians as they could not afford masks. Its former users had so little faith in it that they agreed to ban it at a disarmament conference in 1932.

TANKS

Before the war broke out American farmers had been using tractors with tracks instead of wheels. These spread the load over a greater area, reduce ground pressure and make it possible for the vehicle to cross very muddy ground. When it was suggested that one of these could be covered in thick steel plates and equipped with machine guns, the British Ministry of War dismissed the whole idea as a silly gimmick. Most British generals were cavalry men. Some historians believe that they wanted the war to be won by men charging on horseback and were having difficulty in coming to terms with the fact that this was not going to happen in the age of barbed wire, mud and machine guns. Winston Churchill, the First Lord of the Admiralty, or the Minister in charge of the Navy,

used money from the Navy's budget to develop the weapon until the army agreed to try it out. The prototypes had to be able to go at 6 kph (or 4 mph), cross a 2.5m (8ft) wide trench and climb a short 45 degree slope.

"I went … to witness the official trial of the first machine … The experiment was a complete success, the tank achieved even more than it was asked to accomplish. I can recall the feeling of delighted amazement with which I saw for the first time the ungainly monster, bearing the inscription 'HMS Centipede' on its breast, plough through thick (barbed wire) entanglements, wallow through deep mud and heave its huge bulk over parapets and across trenches. At last, I thought, we have the answer to German machine guns and wire … (General) Sir

William Robertson was also favourably impressed, but Lord Kitchener scoffed as the huge, clumsy creature lumbered and tumbled about, though always moving forward, and expressed the opinion that it would very quickly be knocked out by artillery."
(*War Memoirs of David Lloyd George* page 383)

Tanks were first used in September 1916 when the Battle of the Somme was going badly for Britain. This was premature. The army did not have enough of them, nor had they thought out the best way to use them. Although the tanks were able to crush the barbed wire and cross the German trenches, they did not achieve a breakthrough since many of them broke down, ran out of petrol or got stuck in the mud. Once immobile they were a sitting target for German field guns (light artillery). John Terraine pointed out that:

"...useful as the 1916–1918 tanks were for breaking into enemy positions and saving infantry lives, they were not weapons of exploitation as we saw in World War II. Their 'mobility' over rough ground was often reduced to 1 or 1½ miles per hour; the maximum speed of a Mark IV (1917) was 3.7 mph, of a Mark V (1918) 5 mph and of a 'Whippet', 7 mph. Partly because of this, and for other reasons too, they were extremely vulnerable."
(John Terraine, *The Western Front 1914–1918* page 220)

At Cambrai in November 1917 tanks were used with much more skill. The army had learned that the most important skill of the tank commander is to hide his tank until it is needed. 378 were massed behind the lines and were brought up at night while aircraft flew overhead to drown the noise. The Germans did not expect an attack here as it was part of the carefully prepared Hindenburg line with deep concrete forts and 20 metre wide belts of barbed wire. Once again the tanks easily crushed the wire and penetrated the German defences to a depth of 6 km (4 miles). Because there had been little fighting here the ground was not too badly cut up or muddy. George Coppard recalled:

"From a concealed position on my right a Jerry machine gun opened fire. My hair stood on end as the bullets hissed past me. The gunner was just a trifle too late to get me. There was a tank nearby beginning to move after a stop. I told one of the crew about the machine gun. 'We'll fix the bastard,' he replied, and slowly the tank shuffled round on its tracks and rolled off in the direction of the hostile gun. Then came a fiery burst as the hapless weapon tried to beat off the tank, the bullets clanging and ricocheting. The team crossed … safely, well bucked at this practical demonstration of a tank in action."
(George Coppard, *With a Machine Gun to Cambrai* pages 124–125)

Unfortunately many British soldiers had been transferred to Italy to help the Italians against Austria. There were not enough infantry to follow up and consolidate the tanks' gains. Tanks

Early tanks came in two varieties, male and female. 'Mr Tank' had a small artillery piece protruding from a turret on either side, while 'Mrs Tank' was equipped with scarcely visible machine guns. Later, hermaphrodite tanks were introduced which carried both sorts of weapons.

Unditching beam: The crew could free a stuck tank by placing this wooden beam under the tracks. The tank then climbed out over it.

Fascine: Used to cross trenches

Tracks: These reduce ground pressure and allow the tank to manoeuvre in the mud.

THE TANK

are an offensive weapon and are of little use in defending a position. Cavalry, another offensive force, were sent in and were mown down by machine gun fire. Once again the tanks began to break down, run out of fuel or fall prey to field guns. One German gun took out sixteen tanks. The Germans closed the gap and stalemate returned. At this point the tank seemed such a failure that the Germans did not try to copy it, although they did play around with captured vehicles and experiment with methods of destroying them, for instance by using flame throwers.

Although tanks were initially a failure, they were much better understood by the end of the war and played a vital part in pushing the Germans back in the last few months. Generals learned that tanks should not go too far and that they should have plenty of infantry to consolidate the position before advancing again. By late 1918 they were mechanically more reliable and Renault produced small, faster, lightweight tanks for the French which were very effective against infantry. It had also been discovered that concentrated shelling followed by tanks, supported by aircraft, could break up most defensive formations.

"From a mockery the tanks have become a terrible weapon. Armoured they come rolling on in long lines, more than anything else embodying for us the horror of war.

We do not see the guns that bombard us; the attacking lines of enemy infantry are men like ourselves; but these tanks are machines, their caterpillars run on as endlessly as the war, they

Operating on a slightly wounded man in a regimental aid post by Austin O Spare
(© Imperial War Museum)

are annihilation, they roll without feeling into the craters, and climb up again without stopping, a fleet of roaring, smoke-belching armour-clads, invulnerable steel beasts squashing the dead and the wounded— we shrivel up in our thin skin before them, against their colossal weight our arms are sticks of straw, and our hand grenades matches.

Shells, gas clouds, and flotillas of tanks—shattering, corroding death."
(Erich Maria Remarque, *All Quiet on the Western Front* page 238)

This set the pattern for the Second World War when there was little trench fighting.

AIRCRAFT
Flying machines were a relative novelty in 1914. The first heavier than air machine had been flown by the Wright brothers in Ohio in 1904. Bleriot made the first cross-channel flight in 1909. The army was quick to see the possibilities of aircraft for reconnaissance (spying on enemy troop movements) and artillery spotting. Since artillery shells fell miles from the guns, well out of sight, it was essential to have somebody who could see where they were falling and tell the gunners so that they could correct their aim. Aircraft

were ideal, so the army set up the Royal Flying Corps which became a separate service, the RAF, in 1918. Early aircraft could only carry very limited loads, but as the design improved they were used to bomb ground targets. By the end of the war both sides had built large, four-engined aircraft for the purpose, although these were not used over the trenches. When the war was over they were fitted with basket chairs, instead of bombs, and became the first airliners.

The first aircraft were not armed. When British pilots met a German machine the fliers would wave to each other. Later somebody took a pistol and shot at the enemy, then the observer used a hunting rifle and before long machine guns were being mounted on the aircraft. The fighter was born and in the late stages of the war proved useful for attacking infantry on the ground as well as enemy aircraft.

MEDICAL TECHNOLOGY

The most obvious effect of the developments described above was about nine million deaths and twenty million seriously wounded men. Most of the British soldiers wounded in action were treated in huge tented hospitals where many of them died of blood loss. Perhaps the most significant medical development at this time was that of blood transfusions which the Americans introduced late in the war. Early attempts at this by British doctors failed because they did not know about the need for blood type matching. The war also produced a rapid development in prosthetics, the making of artificial limbs, and in plastic surgery.

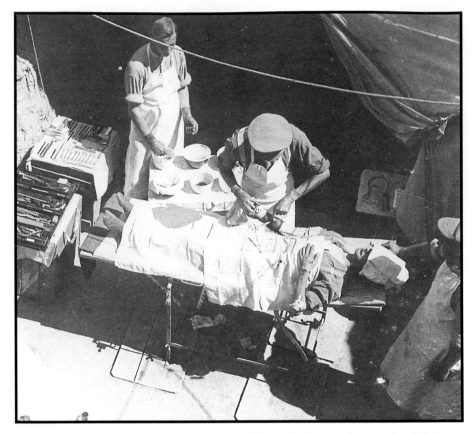

A wounded 'Tommy' is treated in a makeshift medical post close to the fighting
(© Imperial War Museum)

Source

A gas attack described in the novel *All Quiet on the Western Front* by Erich Maria Remarque, a veteran of the Kaiser's army.

"The dull thud of gas-shells mingles with the crashes of the high explosives. A bell sounds between the explosions, gongs and metal clappers warning everyone –Gas –Gas – Gaas ……

These first minutes with the mask decide between life and death: is it air-tight? I remember the awful sights in the hospital: who in day-long suffocation cough up their burned-out lungs in clots. Cautiously the mouth applied to the valve, I breath. The gas still creeps over the ground and sinks into the hollows. Like a big, soft jelly fish it floats into our shell-hole and lolls there obscenely … it is better to crawl out and lie on top than stay where the gas collects most.

Inside my gas-mask my head booms and roars—it is nigh bursting. My lungs are tight, they breath always the same hot, used up air, the veins on my temple are swollen. I feel I am suffocating … I polish the windows. I peer through them, the man there no longer wears his mask. I wait some seconds—he has not collapsed … rattling in my throat I tear mine off too."

One of the strange features of the First World War was that a huge amount of poetry was written about it. Gaelic speaking students will already be familiar with *An Eala Bhan* by Domhnall Ruadh Choruna, probably the finest love poem to emerge from the trenches in any language.

Wilfred Owen (1893 – 1918) was one of the most famous poets of the war. He was against the war from the start but join the Artists Rifles in 1915 because he felt that nobody would take his writing seriously unless he was writing from first-hand experience. He wanted to be a primary source. He was in the trenches from January to June 1917 when he was sent to Craiglochart Hospital, Edinburgh with shell shock and shattered nerves. There he met and formed a close friendship with Siegfried Sassoon, possibly the most famous of the war poets. Owen returned to the front and was killed by machine gun fire, leading his men across the Sambre canal on 4 November 1918. The following poem is about a gas attack. Its last lines mean *It is sweet and honourable to die for your country*. This Latin inscription appeared on many war memorials.

Dulce et Decorum est

Bent double like old beggars under sacks,
Knock-kneed, coughing like hags, we cursed through sludge,
Till on the haunting flares we turned our backs,
And towards our distant rest began to trudge.
Men marched asleep. Many had lost their boots,
But limped on, blood-shod. All went lame, all blind;
Drunk with fatigue; deaf even to the hoots
of gas shells dropping softly behind.

Gas! Gas! Quick boys!—an ecstasy of fumbling,
Fitting the clumsy helmets just in time,
But someone still was yelling out and stumbling
And floundering like a man in fire and lime.
Dim through the misty panes and thick green light,
As under a green sea, I saw him drowning.
In all my dreams, before my helpless sight,
He plunges at me, guttering choking, drowning.

If in some smothering dreams, you too could pace
Behind the wagon that we flung him in,
And watch the white eyes writhing in his face,
His hanging face, like a devil's sick of sin;
If you could hear, at every jolt, the blood
Come gargling from the froth-corrupted lungs,
Obscene as cancer, bitter as the cud
Of vile, incurable sores on innocent tongues,
My friend, you would not tell with such high zest
To children ardent for some desperate glory,
The old Lie: Dulce et Decorum est
Pro Patria Mori.

4 Life and Death in the Trenches

When the war of movement came to an end, the war took on the character for which the First World War is notorious—murderous trench warfare. On the Western Front, Belgian troops manned trenches near their North Sea coast. British and British Empire soldiers occupied the line between the Belgians and the River Somme in France. The French sector stretched from the Somme to the Swiss border.

TRENCH SYSTEMS

Each side had its front line, divided from the enemy by anything from twenty five to several hundred metres of devastation called no-man's-land. Only fragments of buildings and shattered trees remained there. Intense shelling left the area pockmarked with craters which no lunar landscape could hope to rival. Bodies floated in shell holes half-filled with gas-poisoned water. Wounded men often drowned in these craters. Bird song could still occasionally be heard above the din of war and rats scurried about nibbling at corpses. To appear in no-man's-land in daylight was to court almost certain death.

The front line trenches were not built to any fixed architect's plan. Their shape and form depended on the land and whatever materials their builders could find. If the soil was deep enough the trenches might be 2.5 metres (8 to 9 feet) deep so a man could walk upright without getting his head shot off. In wet or rocky ground such depth and security would be impossible.

"… Mr Clark was shot through the head shortly after arriving. … A machine gun swept the breastwork and got him. He died on … the early hours of Christmas Day … a life thrown away because a man was tall. Mr Clark was a giant. I can't understand how the military bosses overlooked the shocking handicap which tall men were under in trench warfare. Surely the artillery was the place for tall chaps …"
(George Coppard, *With a Machine Gun to Cambrai* pages 59–60)

The trenches were not straight but zig-zagged so that the blast and shrapnel from a shell bursting in the trench would be contained between the bends and so kill or maim fewer men. The sides would be reinforced with anything that came to hand or could be brought in—corrugated iron, railway sleepers, sandbags or wickerwork.

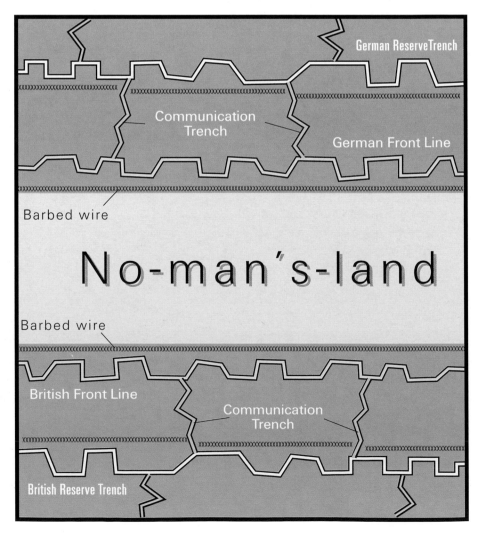

Duckboards were often laid on the bottom in an attempt to create a drier walkway. On the forward side of the trench there was often a small platform called the firestep from where riflemen could defend their trench from attack or sentries could keep watch. Often periscopes were used to observe the enemy since raising one's head above the parapet was not recommended! Sleeping caves, called dugouts, were excavated in the back wall of the trench. Again they were of no fixed pattern. The German trenches were usually much better than those of the French or the British. German soldiers could retire to concrete-lined shelters ten

Highlanders eating by their dugout (© Imperial War Museum)

Oppy Wood by John Nash (© Imperial War Museum)

metres underground with real beds and electric light while the British Tommy, French Poilu[1] or Anzac (Australian /New Zealand Army Corps soldier) crept under a sheet of corrugated iron covered in sandbags and was grateful for the old door, looted from a ruined house, which was his bed. Usually British officers had better accommodation than their men with beds, something which looked like a table and a chair or two. Allied generals did not like the men to get too comfortable as it was assumed that they would soon be moving forward to drive the 'beastly Hun' out of France.

At night, work parties crept out of their trenches and strung barbed wire from steel corkscrew pickets or repaired damage done by shell-fire. Forward

[1]Poilu: French slang for soldier, means hairy

trenches could be dug in no-man's-land, even under fire, by using a shell hole as a starting point.

Behind the front line were the reserve or support trenches where reinforcements waited in case they were needed. The

supports were a fall back line should the front line be taken.

Communication trenches linked front and reserve lines and ran back, often for several kilometres until a point was reached where it was fairly safe to walk in the open. Communi-

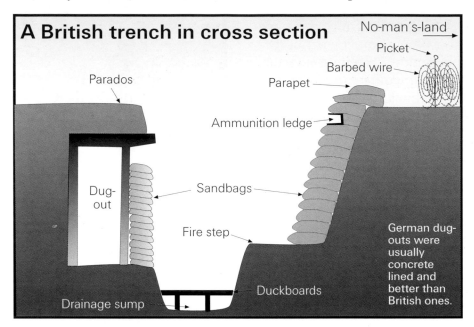

A British trench in cross section

No-man's-land
Picket
Barbed wire
Parados
Parapet
Ammunition ledge
Dug-out
Sandbags
Fire step
Drainage sump
Duckboards

German dugouts were usually concrete lined and better than British ones.

Australian troops in the trenches. Note the Lewis gun, Lee-Enfield rifles and the periscope. (© Imperial War Museum)

cation trenches were frequently extremely muddy. When going up the line Scottish soldiers sometimes removed their kilts and carried them across their packs so that they had warm dry clothes when they got to the front line. This was not so easy with trousers.

CONDITIONS IN THE TRENCHES

Soldiers lived with the constant fear of imminent death. The life expectancy of a 2nd lieutenant in the trenches was only three months. No soldier needed to be reminded that he could be crushed by a collapsing trench, ripped to shreds by shrapnel, cut in half by machine gun fire, gutted by a bayonet, blown apart by high explosive shells, drowned in a shell hole or that he could get a bullet in the brain.

All soldiers believed in fate. The British used to say, 'You can't do anything if a bullet's got your number on it. It's going to get you.' Remarque put it this way:

> "It is just a matter of chance that I am still alive and that I might have been hit. In a bomb-proof dugout I may be smashed to atoms and in the open may survive ten hours' bombardment unscathed. No soldier outlives a thousand chances. But every soldier believes in Chance and trusts his luck."
>
> (Erich Maria Remarque, *All Quiet on the Western Front* page 90)

Artillery bombardments could go on for days on end, with shells whistling or screaming through the air. Cowering in their holes in the ground, the men were showered with soil as they heard and felt the explosions tearing at the tormented earth. Being frightened is very tiring. It also destroys the mind and nervous system. In the early days of the war men who suf-

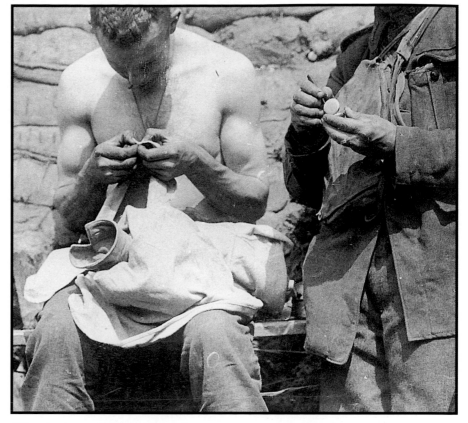

"Chatting' – a soldier hunts for lice (© Imperial War Museum)

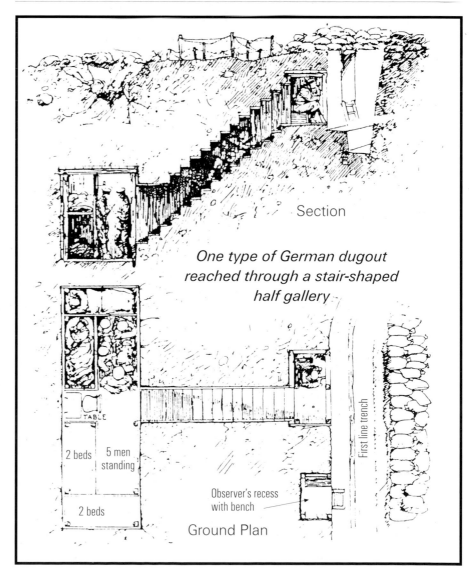

Section

One type of German dugout reached through a stair-shaped half gallery

TABLE

2 beds   5 men standing

2 beds

Observer's recess with bench

Ground Plan

First line trench

fered from nervous breakdowns were dismissed as cowards.

"If any poor devil's nerves got the better of him, and he was found wandering behind the lines, a not infrequent occurrence, it was … a cowardice or desertion case. There was no psychiatric defence available to save him from the firing squad … . They recognised a shell-shock case when a man lost control of his limbs, but what of the man who, although not a raving lunatic, loses control of his will? It is my considered opinion that some men who met their end before a firing squad would willingly have fought the enemy in hand-to-hand combat, but simply could not endure prolonged shell and mortar fire."
(George Coppard, *With a Machine Gun to Cambrai* page 42)

Victims lost control of their limbs and would shake gro-tesquely from head to foot. Some foamed at the mouth or became incontinent. The army eventually set up special hospitals to deal with the victims. Craiglochart in Edinburgh treated officers such as the poets Siegfried Sassoon and Wilfred Owen. Owen spoke of "men whose minds the dead had ravished". Elsewhere electric shocks were administered to sufferers. The effects of shell shock were often long-lasting.

"I was playing cricket a couple of years after the war. Our fast bowler came running in to bowl, a big strong chap. A car backfired in the street outside the ground and he collapsed in a heap, writhing and foaming at the mouth."
(Mr Hughes, French teacher and war veteran, speaking to a class in which the present author was a pupil. c1959)

The soldiers suffered from a variety of physical health problems. It was impossible to keep clean at the front and clothes quickly became louse infested. 'Verminous' soldiers were said to be 'chatty' and spent hours 'chatting' or hunting lice and lice eggs in their clothes. The eggs were often found in the seams.

"A lighted candle applied where they were thickest made them pop like Chinese crackers. After a session of this my face would be covered in blood spots from extra big fellows which had popped too vigorously."
(George Coppard, *With a Machine Gun to Cambrai* page 44)

The kilt had severe disadvantages here as it harboured lice in the folds.

"When we got a few days behind the lines we were sent to the delousing station where we got a special chlorine bath and our clothes were treated. It didn't do a lot of good. You would be chatty again in no time. The best way to treat the

Stretcher bearers. This famous picture gives an impression of the mud at Passchendaele. (© Imperial War Museum)

kilt was to run a hot iron down the pleats. You could hear the eggs bursting ... pop, pop, pop as the iron ran along."
(Old soldier on BBC Radio interview c 1984)

The lice caused horrible itchy sores especially round the neck, wrists and ankles. They also caused outbreaks of deadly diseases like typhus and have been blamed for 'trench fever', a problem which affected both sides. The symptoms were very similar to influenza. Men ran a high fever for three to five days and then felt better.

Much of the land in Flanders, the part of Belgium where the British fought, and Northern France is very flat. The shelling destroyed drainage systems which local farmers had laboured for hundreds, if not thousands, of years to create. The result was mud beyond the powers of our imagination.

"Immediately there came a crackle of bullets and mud was splattered about me as I ran, crawled and dived into shell holes, over bodies, sometimes up to my armpits in water, sometimes crawling on my face along a ridge of slimy mud around a crater ... Exhausted by my efforts, I paused a moment in a shell hole; in a few seconds I felt myself sinking, and struggle as I might I was sucked down until I was firmly gripped round the waist and still being dragged in. The leg of a corpse was sticking out of the side, and frantically I grabbed it; wrenched it off, and casting it down I pulled in a couple of rifles and yelled to the troops in the gunpit to throw me more. Laying them flat I wriggled over them and dropped, half dead, into the wrecked gun position."
(Edwin Campion Vaughan, *Some Desperate Glory: Diary of a Young Infantry Officer, 1917* pages 222–223)

It was virtually impossible for men to keep their feet dry in the muddy trenches. The skin quickly went wrinkly, as it does if you spend too long in the bath or in a swimming pool, but then it died and the flesh went black and started to rot. In extreme cases the flesh round the toes merged into a stinking pulp and amputation was the only solution. Officers were required to inspect their men's feet daily and make sure that they rubbed them with whale oil.

Soldiers who had not brushed their teeth for days on end might suffer from trench mouth. The symptoms were painful and consisted of bleeding gums, ulcers of the mouth and throat and very bad breath.

The army did its best to ensure that the men used trench latrines, usually in the support trenches, rather than defecating in shell holes or in or near the trenches. With hundreds of thousands of soldiers about this was not easy. Drinking water was often hard to get at the front line and sometimes contaminated water from shell holes was drunk causing cholera epidemics. This was a huge problem in Gallipoli, where the Allies fought the Turks in 1914 and 1915. In that campaign more men died of disease than from bullet wounds.

Rats tormented the soldiers and spread disease.

> "The outstanding feature of the Armentières sector was the extraordinary number of rats. The area was infested with them … It was impossible to keep them out of the dugouts even … They grew fat on the food that they had pilfered from us …; they were bloated and loathsome to look on. We were filled with an instinctive hatred of them because … one could not help feeling that they had fed on the dead. We waged ceaseless war on them and, indeed, they were easy prey because owing to their nauseating plumpness they were slow of foot … The officers on their nightly rounds would fire on them with their revolvers, and in the morning it would be a common sight to see disembowelled rats lying among our barbed wire.
>
> We used to tie our food in sandbags, and these we would hang from the rafters of the dugout. The rats would get the food though, and to do so they must have climbed down the string.
>
> One night a rat ran across my face. Unfortunately my mouth happened to be open and the hind legs of the filthy little beast went right in."
> [A Stuart Dolden, *Cannon Fodder (An Infantryman's Life on the Western Front 1914 to 1918)* pages 110–111]

German soldiers lived with the same problems.

> "The rats here are particularly repulsive, they are so fat—the kind we call corpse rats. They have shocking, evil, naked faces, and it is nauseating to see their long, nude tails.
>
> They seem mighty hungry. Almost every man has had his bread gnawed. Kropp wrapped his in his waterproof sheet and put it under his head, but he cannot sleep because they run over his face to get at it. Detering meant to outwit them. He fastened a thin wire to the roof and suspended his bread from it. During the night when he switched on his pocket-torch he saw the wire swinging to and fro. On the bread was riding a fat rat.
>
> … we carefully cut off the bits of bread that the animals have gnawed. The slices … are heaped together in the middle of the floor. Each man takes his spade … Detering, Kropp and Kat hold their pocket-torches ready … we hear the first shuffling and tugging … now is the sound of many little feet … the torches switch on and every man strikes at the heap … The result is good. We toss the bits of rat over the parapet and again lie in wait."
> (Erich Maria Remarque, frontline soldier of the Kaiser's Army, *All Quiet on the Western Front* pages 90–91)

In summer there were other plagues.

> "Flies were a terrible problem. An infantry division had about five thousand to six thousand horses. These horses made forty tons of droppings every day. This was a good breeding ground for flies. One soldier said that the buzzing of the flies drowned the noise of a shell whizzing on the battlefield on a hot day … The flies rose in black clouds from the dead bodies … "
> (Fiona Reynoldson, *War beyond Britain* page 18)

Stuart Dolden remembered:

> "During the time we remained in 'death valley' we were considerably troubled by hundreds of bluebottles; … at one spot as I put my foot down there was a loud buzzing and hundreds of bluebottles flew up. There to my astonishment I saw a face— the face of a dead German. The whole ridge was covered in French and German dead, upon which swarms of bluebottles had settled. These same insects no doubt … were going to settle on our food."
> (A Stuart Dolden, *Cannon Fodder* page 86)

The Smell

Many survivors of the war were very reluctant to talk about it later. They would say that it was impossible for anyone to begin to understand what it had been like unless they had been there. The smell, they said, was indescribable. Erich Maria Remarque tried.

> "The days are hot and the dead lie unburied. We cannot fetch them all in, if we did we should not know what to do with them. The shells will bury them. Many have bellies swollen up like balloons. They hiss, belch and make movements. The gas in them makes noises. The sky is blue and without clouds. In the evening it grows sultry and the heat rises from the earth. When the wind blows towards us it brings the smell of blood, which is very heavy and sweet. This deadly exhalation from the shell-holes seems to be a mixture of chloroform and putrefaction, and fills us with nausea and retching."
> (Erich Maria Remarque, *All Quiet on the Western Front* page 110)

In 1916 the Germans attacked the French forts at Verdun. Twenty three million shells were fired and about 650,000 men were killed. More than one-third of these were never formally buried. The shells tossed their remains around and the whole place stank of death—200,000 men rotting in the open. The clothes of the living and the food they ate carried the stink of rotting flesh. Old soldiers recalled the smell of cordite from the guns, sweat, bacon frying on fires lit from broken up ammunition boxes and decaying flesh. Some said they could smell it in their dreams.

MILITARY JUSTICE

British troops were governed by a code of discipline which was strict, often brutal and not always even-handed. For minor offences, such as not keeping a rifle clean, they could be subjected to No. 1 Field Punishment. The offender would be tied to the wheel of a gun carriage or to a wooden cross and left in the cold for several hours, often rather too close to the front line.

For more serious offences, a spell in military prison with hard labour carried no guarantee of survival. A worn-out sentry who fell asleep at his post might be sentenced to death by the firing squad, as might the shell-shock victim who finally cracked and ran away, a deserter, or one who showed cowardice in the face of the enemy.

"Upwards of 300 British soldiers were shot by court martial verdicts between 1914 and 1918 and this figure must be regarded as one that excludes those dispatched in the heat of battle pour encourager les autres and without the formalities of charges and pleas. It excludes, too, the hapless Chinese labour corps strikers shot down wholesale by military police in the Calais base strike of 1917."
(*They also Fell: British Battlefield Justice, The Scotsman* 12 November 1983)

The German general, Ludendorff, is said to have envied the freedom British commanders had to discipline their men in this way. The Australians and New Zealanders, often acknowledged to be the cream of the fighting force of the British Empire, had no need of such a penalty to get them to fight.

"Sylvia Pankhurst, suffragette and pacifist, took up the case of several East London families who had been notified of their sons' executions, for not until late 1917 was it seen fit to inform next of kin that executed soldiers had simply been killed in action ... After the armistice Labour MPs ... began a campaign to delete the death penalty for disciplinary offences from military law. Ernest Thurtle, an ex-soldier, ... led

The Ypres Salient at night by Paul Nash (© *Imperial War Museum*)

this campaign in Parliament … he drew upon some terrible recollections confided in him by … soldiers who had taken part in executions. One … concerns … a sergeant and two corporals who claimed in their defence to have retreated from an attack on the order of an officer who was himself killed in it. Their defence got them nowhere, and Thurtle's correspondent described the outcome …

'A motor ambulance arrives conveying the doomed men. Manacled and blindfolded they are helped out and tied up to stakes. Over each man's heart is placed an envelope. The firing parties, twelve to each, align their rifles on the envelopes. The officer in charge holds his stick aloft, and as it falls thirty six bullets usher three of Kitchener's men to the great unknown. I helped to clear the traces of that triple murder. I took the posts down. I helped the bodies to their last resting place. I collected the blood-soaked straw and burned it. I took all their personal belongings from the dead men's tunics—a few letters, a pipe, some fags. I could tell you of the silence of the military police after reading one letter from a little girl to her 'dear daddy,' of the blood-soaked snow that horrified the French peasants, of the chaplain's confession that braver men he had never met than those three he had prayed with just before the fatal dawn.' "

(*They also Fell: British Battlefield Justice, The Scotsman* 12 November 1983)

Thirty five of those executed were Scots. Officers whose nerves failed them were less likely to be shot than 'other ranks'. Campaigns for pardons by the families of those executed continues to the present day. Court martial records will not become available to historians until one hundred years after the event. This is said to protect the families concerned,

A wounded soldier with his holed helmet. "It's a matter of luck that I am still alive." (© Imperial War Museum)

but some suspect a cover-up of less than fair courts martial.

THE INFANTRYMAN'S ROUTINE

There were many different types of soldier within the army. Engineers, or sappers, repaired bridges and roads and sometimes dug trenches. Artillery soldiers manned the big guns. Signallers ran telephone lines to carry messages to the trenches. Staff officers assisted the generals in planning and organising everything. Generals usually lived in and worked from large mansion houses, or châteaux, borrowed from French landowners. Ordinary soldiers' resentment of them sometimes bordered on hatred. See *the General* below.) It was said that they ate well, never lacked good French wine, slept in comfortable, clean, safe beds and rarely went close enough to the front to see the results of their work.

Below is an outline of the routine of the infantry regiments.

Infantry regiments on the Western Front would rotate between a spell behind the lines, the reserve trenches and the front line trenches.

Behind the lines where the British fought at Ypres in Belgium there were camps in villages like Poperinge, affectionately known as 'Pop'. Here the soldiers were deloused, got some rest and ate better food. Boxing and football matches were organised. Shows and concerts were laid on. The Scottish comic and singer, Harry Lauder, whose own son was killed, visited the front and entertained the men. Less popular were training and drill sessions. The men would also get a chance to go into the villages and refresh themselves in

The General
by Siegfried Sassoon

"Good morning; good morning!" the General said
When we met him last week on our way to the line.
Now the soldiers he smiled at are most of 'em dead
And we're cursing his staff for incompetent swine.
"He's a cheery old card," grunted Harry to Jack
As they slogged up to Arras with rifle and pack.
But he did for them both with his plan of attack.

Siegfried Sassoon was an officer of the PBI, poor bloody infantry, as they called themselves. They made up the majority of the soldiers and they did most of the dying.

an estaminêt or café-bar. Numerous brothels sprang up, some of which were unofficially designated for officer use only.

After about fourteen days behind the lines the regiment would spend eight days in reserve, ready to move into the trenches immediately should the Germans attack. Next they would move up into the reserve or support trenches which were only marginally less dangerous than the front line. On the way up they would pass numerous graveyards with makeshift wooden crosses which were replaced after the war with uniform gravestones in white Cotswold limestone. If they were moving up for a big attack, or 'push', they might notice fields of freshly dug graves and piles of crude wooden coffins waiting to be filled. The army tried to plan for everything. There would also be huge piles of shells and other supplies. After perhaps four days in the supports they would move into the front line. If they survived that for another four days they would then get back to the delousing stations. Enemy action could play havoc with the rotation and sometimes soldiers spent much longer at the front. For instance, the Black Watch once served for forty eight days without a break.

Dawn was the most dangerous time at the front line as most attacks were timed to take place then to take the enemy by surprise. Dawn attacks were good for the British as the Germans had the light behind them and could not see their enemy so easily. Usually all front line soldiers would be ordered to 'stand to' just before dawn, rifles at the ready, in case of an attack. When the danger had passed they would be 'stood down' and

could begin to brew up some tea on primus stoves or on a fire lit from scrap timber from ruined houses or broken ammunition boxes. The smell of bacon frying would waft along the trench. From late 1915 onwards the army tried to send huge pots of hot food up to the front line from field kitchens but often they did not get through.

During the day fatigue parties strengthened and repaired trenches. They had to work with great caution as both sides had snipers placed to take out anybody careless enough to show his head for an instant. Also,

> "There were latrines at intervals along the line, which generally took the form of a small cul-de-sac cut in the back of the trench. The sites were shifted when necessary, as Jerry snipers watched them very closely for the careless. Many a poor Tommy met his end in a latrine sap."
> (George Coppard, *With a Machine Gun to Cambrai* page 23)

Highland gamekeepers were often used as snipers by Scottish regiments as they were used to taking down a deer with a headshot at four hundred yards. The casualty rate among these marksmen was high as there was always another sniper on the lookout for them. During the day sentries watched the enemy line through home-made periscopes.

Days in the trenches could be very monotonous and boring, despite the ever present danger. Men would write letters or field postcards home. These had to be read by a censor who would blank out any information which could be of interest to a spy. Many soldiers kept diaries, although this was against King's Regulations as German raiding

parties might find useful information in the diary kept by a prisoner. Games of cards and chess went on endlessly.

In quiet areas of the line, the soldiers on both sides tried to avoid doing anything which might annoy the enemy thus leading to a bout of pointless shelling and bloodshed. The British, however, were incorrigible tunnellers, always undermining the German lines and making them feel very uneasy. Every so often they would machine gun the sandbags on the British parapet to see what they contained. If white chalk came spilling out it showed that a Mining Company was busy in the subsoil. Naturally the 'straffing' of their position was unnerving, but it tended to cause relatively few casualties.

Night-time was the most hazardous. Major attacks were never launched at night as it would be impossible for large numbers to find their way quietly through no-man's-land, but both sides regularly sent out raiding parties. The object of this was usually to take a few prisoners for interrogation. Staff officers liked to know where the enemy's best and weakest troops were. The British knew that the Prussian Guards were much more determined than the Saxons who did not really want to be in the war anyway. For their part, German regiments had been known to refuse to go into the line against the Australians and General Ludendorff rated the Scots as the best infantry at the disposal of the British. Attacks against a weak regiment were more likely to succeed. Raiding parties crept across no-man's-land, trying to avoid being spotted by sentries, hiding in shell holes when magnesium flares or star

Stew in the trenches (© Imperial War Museum)

shells bathed the battlefield in glaring white light. Leaping into the enemy's trench, they bayonetted or shot those they could not take prisoner before retreating, leaving behind their own dead and badly wounded.

At night, also, fatigue parties crept out to work in front of their line. Standing upright in the open, shielded only by darkness, they screwed in long metal corkscrews called barbed wire pickets and strengthened their wire. Sometimes they recovered the bodies of fallen comrades for burial or crawled out to bring in a wounded man. While some soldiers tried to sleep, sentries stood alert, peering out into the darkness. Going to sleep while on guard was an offence which carried the death penalty.

How well were the soldiers fed?

We know from various sources that food became a major problem for the German army.

> "With us food is pretty scarce and none too good at that—turnips cut into six pieces and boiled in water, and unwashed carrot tops—mouldy potatoes are tit bits, and the chief luxury is a thin rice soup in which float little bits of beef-sinew, but these are cut up so small that they take a lot of finding. Everything gets eaten … "
> (Erich Maria Remarque, *All Quiet on the Western Front* pages 162–163)

British soldiers did not go hungry unless enemy action prevented supplies getting through. Although we would not envy them their diet, it has to be borne in mind that the working-class soldiers, at any rate, were accustomed to a poor diet and probably did not feel too badly off. Perhaps army ideas of food hygiene would fall a little short of those of your Home Economics teacher, however.

> "Wrapping loose rations such as tea, cheese and meat was not considered necessary, all being tipped into a sandbag, a ghastly mix-up resulting. In wet weather their condition was unbelievable … "
> (George Coppard, *With a Machine Gun to Cambrai* page 43)

Bread and cheese were reasonably plentiful as was the dreaded army plum and apple jam which the men believed was bulked out with turnips, potatoes and sawdust. The poet, Robert Graves, developed an obsessive hatred of the 'war profiteer' who made the jam for the War Department. After the war he wrote a novel, *An Ancient Castle*, in which the villain was an evil jam maker. Men fantasised about strawberry jam. Tins of Argentinean 'bully beef' could be eaten cold or made into a stew. Few of us, today, would share George Coppard's enthusiasm for maconochie.

> "Maconochie, a 'dinner in a tin', was my favourite and I could polish one off with gusto, but the usual share out was one tin for four men ... I don't ever recollect receiving an apple or an orange as part of my rations in France."

Maconochie was tinned stew, but stewed what?

> "Gruesome and distasteful though it was, we augmented our supplies from the dead ... A tin of bully beef in a dead man's pack can't help him, nor can a packet of cigarettes."
> (George Coppard, *With a Machine Gun to Cambrai* page 85)

Water was sent to the front in jerrycans and was so heavily chlorinated to kill germs that it gave a strange taste to the tea. Other flavours were possible:

> "Tea was all we had that night in Poelcapelle. There was no chance of getting the rations up ... We were just crouched in shell holes waiting, and there was one little chap. He made tea all night long, and kept nipping out to get water from flooded ground behind us and heating it up as best he could. Every half hour he'd say, 'There you are Tommy, a drop of tea.' It wasn't very hot, but it kept us going. The next morning when it got light he looked over the side where he'd got the water and it was a bleeding shell hole, and there was a dead Jerry in it and blood all floating around. We'd had that and all in our tea ... We seemed to have no ill effects and we had other things to worry about ..."
> (Sgt. T Berry, DCM speaking to Lyn MacDonald for *They Called it Passchendaele*)

This delightful little story gives an insight into how men kept going and even survived the trenches. Comradeship was vital for no man could survive on his own. The little teamaker gave himself something to do, kept his mind off reality and got himself through the night by brewing up tea for his mates. Drinking the tea kept them going. In return they would look out for him. After the war many soldiers found they had become addicted to comradeship. They needed to be part of a group and to experience the mutual support. They could no longer relate to their families or former friends who had not experienced the hell of war.

The monument to the 51st Highland Division at Beaumont Hamel on the Somme bears the inscription

Là a' Bhlàir
's math na càirdean

Roughly translated from the original Gaelic it means 'Friends are good on the day of battle'—something which can have many meanings.

The monument to the 51st Highland Division at Beaumont Hamel on the Somme.

Trench Fighting

Once the system of trenches had been established, generals on both sides looked for ways to achieve a breakthrough. They wanted to get through the lines of enemy trenches into the open and undamaged land beyond, ending the stalemate of the trenches and restoring a war of movement. The British Commander, Field Marshall Haig, had a cavalry background and wanted conditions where his horsemen could get back into action.

As we have seen, the technology of war favoured defence, not attack. Until the final stages of the war, all offensives failed and no breakthrough was achieved. The Germans quickly realised that they would lose more men if they attacked than if they defended and, between April 1915 and March 1918, launched only one major offensive—against the French at Verdun in 1916.

Although the British and the French also failed to break through, they continued to launch attacks and offensives in an attempt to drive the enemy from French and Belgian soil. They knew that they had more men than the Germans. It has been claimed that they continued to attack, knowing that the Germans would run out of men first. The Allies could lose ten men for every seven Germans they killed. This is called a war of attrition, slowly grinding down the enemy by constant attacks. Men come to be seen as

We are making a new world by Paul Nash *(© Imperial War Museum)*

Above: *Dead Germans in a trench* by Sir William Orpen *(© Imperial War Museum)*

Below: *Wire and dead Australians (© Imperial War Museum)*

resources to be used up, as numbers rather than as individuals. Historians who defend Field Marshall Haig, the British Commander, claim that he never launched an attack purely to wear down the enemy.

Attacks on the enemy by and large all followed the same pattern. First of all the enemy trenches would be bombarded by artillery to soften them up. This alerted them to the fact that an attack was coming. During the night, work parties did their best to remove the barbed wire from in front of their own trenches.Before dawn the attackers massed in the front line with bayonets fixed. Dawn came. The artillery ceased firing. A whistle blew and the men went 'over the top', often into a hail of rifle and machine gun fire.

If enough men made it across no-man's-land and through the enemy wire they leapt into the front line trench, killing those who resisted and possibly taking prisoner those who did not. Hand grenades would be hurled into dugouts to 'clean them out'. A second wave of attackers might be sent on to tackle the reserve trench while the first wave attempted to excavate a fire step on the rear wall of the captured line. Frequently, a counterattack would restore the trench to its original owners. If not, the victors had the satisfaction of knowing that they had captured a few hundred yards of mud.

When soldiers successfully captured an enemy trench they often lost it almost immediately. If a counterattack could be mounted within about twenty minutes, the trench could be retaken before a firestep could be

(continued on page 46)

THE BATTLE

To get an idea of what a major trench battle was like we shall focus on one of these, the Battle of the Somme in 1916.

French troops at the Battle of the Somme.

IN 1915, the Somme was chosen for an offensive because it was an area where the British and French could attack in strength together. When the Germans attacked the French at Verdun in February 1916, the French contribution to the offensive had to be cut from forty to five divisions. The purpose of the offensive then became to take the pressure off the French at Verdun, but by June this was no longer necessary as the Germans had given up. Still the offensive went ahead.

"… the Somme was peculiarly unsuited as an object of attack. The Germans everywhere occupied the crests of the hills; the attackers had to fight their way uphill against a concealed enemy. There had been no previous fighting on a serious scale, and the German defences had long been neglected. But the British High Command, unlike the French and the Germans, believed in keeping their men on their toes by constant activity. These raids, which had no strategic purpose, not only wasted lives. They also provoked the Germans into strengthening their defences … By the summer of 1916, the German front line was heavily covered by barbed wire. Behind it was a second line, equally strong … and the Germans had dugouts forty feet deep complete with every convenience, which made them secure from the heaviest bombardment."
(AJP Taylor, *The First World War* pages 131–132)

The dugouts were concrete lined. German machine gun crews practised carrying their weapons up from the dugouts and setting them up so that they could be firing within three minutes of an artillery bombardment ending.

The British plan was simple. British artillery stood wheel to wheel along an 18 mile (29km) front and blasted the Germans for seven days and nights. Shrapnel shells were used in an attempt to cut the wire. The noise of the guns could be heard in London. In places they had dug tunnels or 'mines' under the German lines and packed them with up to thirty tons of high explosives. At 7.30 am. on 1 July the artillery ceased firing and the mines were blown, creating huge craters filled with toxic fumes.

The generals did not really trust the soldiers, who were not professional soldiers, but men who had volunteered in the excitement of the early days of the war. If they were allowed to run they would get out of line, so 'Kitchener's army' was ordered to walk across no-man's-land and occupy the remains of the German line. Few Germans were expected to have survived. Some officers gave their men footballs to kick in front of them as they walked.

When the shelling ended the German machine gun crews rushed up from their deep shelters. Their trenches had all but disappeared but the wire was largely intact. They set up their weapons and began to mow down the advancing British.

"Though their one chance was speed, they were weighed down with 66lbs (30kg) of equip-

OF THE SOMME

ment, and often more—field telephones, carrier pigeons, picks and shovels ... The bullets ran across the line in a steady spray. The first British line faltered and fell, a second followed it, a third and then a fourth, all to no avail. By the end of the afternoon the survivors were back in their trenches."
(AJP Taylor, *The First World War* page 136)

Of all the divisions of the British army, only the Ulster Division captured its day one objective. In the first ten minutes 12,000 men

were killed or badly wounded. There were 60,000 casualties, of whom 20,000 had been killed, on that first day. These were the heaviest losses ever suffered in a single day by the British army, or indeed any army, in that war.

Haig carried on stubbornly, believing that German resistance was about to collapse. In September he made a premature attack with tanks before he had enough to allow him to use them to real effect.

The rain set in and the heavy clay soil of the Somme was churned into the most unimaginable mud. When failure was finally accepted on 13 November, the British had suffered some 420,000 casualties, the French 200,000 and the Germans 450,000. German casualties were unnecessarily high since Falkenhayn, their commander, often ordered them to counterattack and recapture wrecked trenches.

John Terraine's view of the Somme is different from AJP Taylor's.

"I make no bones about my assessment that the Battle of the Somme was a British victory. I base this on Ludendorff's statement that by the end of the year 'the (German) Army had been fought to a standstill and was utterly worn out'—coupled with Hindenburg's warning to the German Chancellor ... 'we must spare the troops a second Somme battle.' "
(John Terraine, *Douglas Haig, The Educated Soldier* page XV)

This photograph shows the Canadian front line at Beaumont Hamel on the Somme as it is today. Clearly visible is a communication trench, the front line, an advanced trench and many shell holes. The German front line was in the distance, marked by the trees, at 'Y Ravine'. At this point on the first day of the Somme the Newfoundland Regiment was cut to ribbons. This area is preserved as a memorial to them.

created facing the enemy on what had been the back wall of the trench.

Trench fighting was often vicious.

"Something moves in the corner of the bay. It is a German … I lunge forward, aiming at his stomach. It is a lightning, instinctive move … I become insane. I want to strike again and again but I cannot. My bayonet does not come clear. I pull, tug, jerk. It does not come out. It is caught between his ribs. The bones grip my blade. I cannot withdraw.

Of a sudden I hear him shriek … We are facing each other—four feet of space separates us. His eyes are distended; … and look as if they will leap from their sockets … his mouth … opens and shuts like a fish out of water. His hands grasp the barrel of my rifle and he joins me in the effort to withdraw …

He looks at me piteously. I put my foot against his body and try to kick him off. He shrieks into my face … I feel I will go insane if I stay in this hole much longer …

It is too much for me. Suddenly I drop the butt of my rifle … I start to run down the bay. A few steps and I turn the corner … I think I hear voices. In a flash I remember that I am unarmed … If they … find me they will stab me just as I stabbed him—and maybe in the ribs too.

He is propped up against the parados … My tugging and pulling works the blade in his insides. Again those horrible shrieks!

I think. I can get out of this if I unfasten the bayonet from the rifle. But I cannot go through with the plan, for the blade is in up to the hilt and the wound … is now a gaping hole. I cannot put my hand there.

Suddenly I remember what I must do. I turn round and pull my breech lock back. The click sounds sharp and clear. He stops his screaming. He looks at me silently now. He knows what I am going to do.

A white Very light soars over our heads … I see his boyish face. He looks like a Saxon … fair …

I pull the trigger. There is a loud report. The blade at the end of my rifle snaps in two … He lies still.

I am free."
(Charles Yale Harrison, *Generals Die in Bed*)

Paths of Glory by CRW Nevinson—*This painting was suppressed by the government as it depicted dead soldiers.*
(© *Imperial War Museum*)

LIONS LED BY DONKEYS?

In 1915 Ludendorff remarked to his fellow German general, Hoffmann, that the British soldiers fought like lions. "True," said Hoffmann, "but they are lions led by donkeys!" From this came a commonly held belief that the casualties of the Great War were caused by generals who were at best unimaginative and at worst stupid and incompetent. A Scot, Field Marshall Sir Douglas Haig, commanded the British army for longer than any other general during the war and has come in for most of the criticism.

> "He was as stubborn as a donkey, as unthinking as a donkey, as inarticulate as a donkey. So Haig was in fact the worst donkey on the British side of the war."

"He didn't ever go up to the front line. He didn't go into the trenches and dirty his boots. Haig had no comprehension of what he was sending men into. A great commander knows exactly what he is sending his men into, as later commanders, like Montgomery, did."

"Haig's attitude to technology was virtually nil. He didn't understand technology. The horse was always what mattered to him."
(Dr John Laffin, an Australian historian on *TimeWatch* BBC2)

Haig's opponents dwell on the fact that he operated from the comfort of the Château de Beaurepaire, 40 miles behind the lines. They maintain that he carried on with the offensives on the Somme (1916) and Passchendaele (1917) long after

it was obvious that they had no hope of success.

His defenders do not deny he had faults. He was not good at oral communication and sometimes failed to correct mistakes he saw others making, but "Haig was far from the idiot of popular myth and the fact that his armies won the greatest series of victories in British Military history means he must be taken seriously as a commander."
(Dr Gary Sheffield, Royal Military Academy, Sandhurst on *TimeWatch*)

Haig, like all the other generals on both sides, was fighting a new type of war with weapons of awesome power, which were mass-produced by the new industrial economies. Many mistakes would be made before the

Over the top by John Nash (© *Imperial War Museum*)

commanders adapted to these weapons and learned how to use them. Haig's defenders claim that he adapted first.

It is agreed that he should have called off the Somme and Passchendaele offensives, but he was misled by over-optimistic intelligence reports to the effect that the Germans were about to crack.

> "One of the myths surrounding Sir Douglas Haig is that, because he was so fond of the cavalry, he must have simply been an old fuddy duddy, always looking back; always resistant to innovation and new weapons. Now this is quite untrue. Haig would welcome any weapon that forwarded his cause ... From the start Haig was enthusiastic about tanks ... but he didn't believe it was the wonder weapon that would win the war. Why didn't the supposedly far-sighted German commanders pick up on the tank?"
> (Professor Trevor Wilson, University of Adelaide on *TimeWatch*)

John Terraine agrees with this view:

> "Work began on tanks in March 1915 ...; without seeing them, Lord Haig was counting on achieving 'decisive results' from the use of 150 of them ... Haig asked for ... 1,000 of them in September 1916 despite the equivocal character of their first performance."
> (John Terraine, *The Western Front 1914–1918* page 220)

> "The simple fact is that fighting that sort of warfare casualties are bound to be heavy. When you look at casualty rates in the Second World War, at least in the 1944–45 campaign, casualty rates equalled or exceeded those of the Western Front. There is no evidence that British losses in the First World War were disproportionately higher than those of our allies, the French, or of our enemies, the Germans."
> (Dr Gary Sheffield on *TimeWatch*)

> "The Somme and Third Ypres were, without question, costly battles—the costliest the British Army has ever fought. They were likely to be, seeing that in both it was engaging the main body of the main enemy ... Fighting the main body of the German army has always been a bloody and exhausting business; the French had to do it from August 1914 until July 1916, and it cost them about 2.25 million casualties; the Russians did it from June 1941 to May 1945 and their casualties were appalling (about 13 million). It would, in my opinion, have been a miracle ... if British casualties had not been very high indeed ..."
> (John Terraine, *Douglas Haig: The Educated Soldier* page xvi)

When the Germans, under Ludendorff, launched their spring offensive in 1918 they pushed the British back forty miles, but got too far ahead of their supplies and artillery and lost one million men, twice Haig's losses on the Somme. Were the generals of all nations asinine? By mid-1918 Haig had learned how to use men, artillery, tanks and aircraft in combination to push the Germans back slowly, stage by stage.

> "This was an extremely horrible war with massive losses and therefore a war which required a commander who could withstand those losses; a commander who had the stubbornness and determination and perhaps even the insensitivity to not be affected by the losses."
> (Dr Gerald de Groot, St Andrews University on *TimeWatch*)

Indeed not all Germans would have applied Hoffmann's verdict on British generals to Haig.

> "Field Marshall Haig is certainly one of the ablest generals in contemporary England and like the majority of able Britons he is of Scottish descent. ... there is very strict discipline under his command. He is a serious and persistent worker and apparently the best man Great Britain has at present to set against her enemies. That his energy and eagerness to attack have not proved equal to the German art of defence will evoke the highest satisfaction all over Germany."
> (the German newspaper *Rheinisch-Westfalische Zeitung*, obtained by *The Times* via the neutral Netherlands and reprinted on 10 May 1917)

> "He never doubted himself and he never doubted the British army. He had the determination to see things through and when other people started to buckle at the knees he held them up."
> (John Hussey, military historian on *TimeWatch*)

Douglas Haig died in 1928 and was buried in Dryburgh Abbey in the Scottish Borders.

6 The Home Front

The First World War was a total war. This means that the governments involved tried to use everybody under their authority. The war was not just between uniformed soldiers and sailors but between the whole population of each of the warring states. Highland children could be used to gather sphagnum moss from bogs on the hills to fill the field dressings issued to each soldier in case he was wounded. Women could work in factories making shells to kill enemy soldiers. Old age pensioners could grow food on patches of waste ground to feed the women shell makers. Logically this means that women, children, old people and civilians generally became 'legitimate targets' who could be killed when the chance arose, just the same as the men in uniform.

ATTACKS ON CIVILIANS

For centuries Britain had considered herself to be immune to foreign attack. It therefore came as a huge shock when German battle-cruisers bombarded Scarborough, Yarmouth and Hartlepool in late 1914, killing one hundred and twenty seven civilians and wrecking many homes. The navy took action to guard against a recurrence of these attacks, but British civilians continued to face death at home. Germany used both fixed wing aircraft and airships, called zeppelins, to bomb British cities. Fixed wing aircraft,

like the Gotha bomber, were relatively fast but could only carry a small payload of bombs and had a very limited operational range. The zeppelin had a huge canvas-covered metal frame and was filled with hydrogen. (See page 50.) It was slow (55 mph) but could fly at 10,000 feet for 60 hours and could drop three tons of bombs on the city below. Being closest to the continent, London bore the brunt of these attacks, but cities as far afield as Glasgow and Newcastle also had a taste of 20th century technology in action. One airman recalled:

> "I joined the Royal Flying Corps in 1916 and was trained as a fighter pilot. Our casualties were dreadful and the whole squadron became exhausted. We were sent back to London to rest. By day we trained young pilots and by night we flew over London looking for zepps. We used tracer bullets (which glow white hot as they fly through the air) in the hope that they would ignite the hydrogen inside the airframe. Zepps were huge, slow and easy to hit but usually the bullets went straight through and out the other side. Occasionally one might hit a strut, cause a spark and the whole thing would explode. Eventually they decided we had had enough of a rest and sent us back to France."
> (Ronnie Black RFC, of Appin, Argyll in conversation with the author c. 1970)

The introduction of incendiary bullets made zeppelins much easier to destroy.

These raids could be justified as attacks on factories producing weapons or on the civilians supporting the war effort. Bombing of civilian targets became a feature of twentieth century warfare but a number of characteristics of this form of warfare quickly became apparent. Extensive damage was inflicted on property, but those who crawled out from the wreckage of their homes tended to be very angry rather than being terrified into submission. Bombing stiffened civilian resolve —rather than break its spirit. It is estimated that zeppelins killed 556 civilians and injured another 1,358, not nearly enough to have any impact on the war effort.

Gotha bombers began attacking the southeast of England in May 1917 and had killed eight hundred civilians by the end of the war causing terror, anger and misery but having no real effect on the outcome of the war.

The Germans were not alone in killing women and children. Although the British preferred to starve them with an effective blockade, we also used bombing. By the end of the war large four-engined bombers such as the DH4 were bombing German towns from bases in France. When the war was over, nobody knew quite what to do with these monsters until somebody had the idea of filling them with wickerwork seats and creating the first airliners.

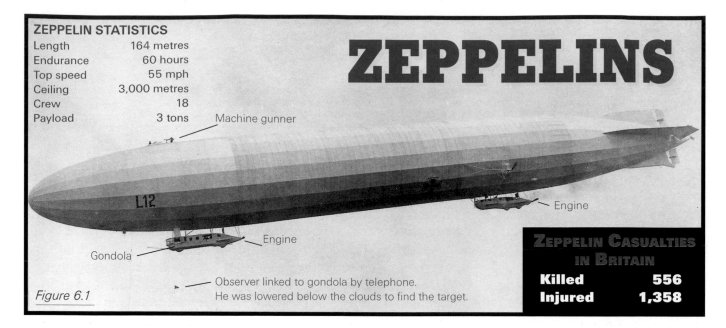

ZEPPELIN STATISTICS

Length	164 metres
Endurance	60 hours
Top speed	55 mph
Ceiling	3,000 metres
Crew	18
Payload	3 tons

Machine gunner

Engine

Gondola

Engine

Observer linked to gondola by telephone.
He was lowered below the clouds to find the target.

Figure 6.1

ZEPPELIN CASUALTIES IN BRITAIN

Killed	556
Injured	1,358

Blockade and Counterblockade

Britain is an island. In war this is a great strength, but potentially also a great weakness. In 1914 Britain produced only 40% of the food it consumed, the rest being imported. It arrived by sea, in ships. Germany readily succumbed to the temptation to try to starve Britain into submission. Since her surface fleet was small by British standards she had to use new technology, namely the submarine. These craft had emerged about the turn of the century and were enthusiastically adopted by the Germans as a cheap and effective way to counter Britain's naval power.

German submarines were able to enter British waters undetected, on the surface by night, submerged by day. In February 1915 the Germans declared the waters round Britain to be a war zone where any vessel, naval or merchant, British or neutral, could be sunk by torpedo or gunfire. By October 1915, when Germany called off her first U-boat campaign, 900,000 tons of British shipping had been sunk. However, British shipyards had replaced this with 2,000,000 tons of new vessels while Germany had lost fifteen of her thirty five U-boats. The Germans had also upset the Americans by sinking the British liner, Lusitania, off Ireland in May with the loss of 1,198 lives, including 128 American citizens. This is, of course, another example of total war and attacks on civilians. The food shortages

German U-Boat

Retractable telescopic periscope

Wires to prevent fouling on nets and cables

Conning tower

Length	119 feet
Beam	14 feet
Crew	23 men

Engines: Diesel for surface travel and recharging electric batteries for underwater travel.

Stabiliser

Two 19.7 inch torpedo tubes

Prop

Rudder

Ballast tanks—flood with water to submerge, pump out to surface

Figure 6.2

which had appeared in Britain were due as much to ships carrying war supplies instead of food, as they were to the U-boats.

By March 1916 Germany's U-boat fleet had expanded to almost four hundred submarines. A new campaign of "unrestricted submarine warfare" began with deadly effect. By August 1917, 1,500,000 tons of British merchant shipping had gone to the bottom, together with many of their civilian crew. Britain was losing ships faster than they could be built and food shortages became serious. At one stage only four days' supply of sugar remained and a few weeks' worth of wheat flour.

The U-boat, however, did not win the war for Germany. The sinking of passenger ships, such as the SS Sussex in the Channel in March 1916, carrying US citizens, was a major factor in the USA's declaration of war in April 1917. In June that year merchant ships started to sail in convoy with an escort of warships to protect them. This dramatically reduced losses.

In Britain various measures were taken to prevent starvation.

The Corn Production Act: 1917

British farmers were paid subsidies to plough up pasture land and plant crops such as potatoes and wheat which were rich in carbohydrate and,therefore, energy. The aim was to feed people plenty of starch so that they would feel full, have energy to work and so not complain.

Allotments: Town councils were encouraged to allocate patches of wasteland to townspeople to grow vegetables. Football fields and golf courses were dug up and rose beds and lawns were replaced by potato patches.

Substitute Foods: People became accustomed to margarine instead of butter and to eating grey bread made partly from flour and partly from potato. Nobody liked dried egg but they ate it nevertheless. In Germany similar ideas were tried. Acorns were roasted, ground up and sold as coffee. Nobody was fooled!

GIRL POWER

British farming was in a poor state at the start of the war having lost much of the home market to imports from the USA, Canada, Australia, New Zealand and Argentina. Now it was called upon to replace these imports at a time when many farm workers had joined the army and gone off to fight. The labour shortfall was met by the creation of the Women's Land Army. Young women, often from prosperous city families, were recruited into a special corps. Uniformed in long leather boots and knee breeches, they were sent off to work on the land where they quickly overcame most doubts about their ability to do a man's job. Many stories are told of the often cruel tricks that were played on them in their early days by wily old farmers, but in the end they proved invaluable and saved the country from starvation.

RATIONING

The shortage of many forms of food led to long queues at the shops and rapidly rising prices. At one time 4,000 people were reported to be waiting outside a London butcher's shop. The poorest suffered the most and there was a danger that hunger would divide the nation and break national morale. The problem became acute during the second U-boat campaign and in December 1917 official rationing was finally introduced after voluntary schemes had failed. Not all foodstuffs were affected. Rationing began with sugar but was later extended to meat, lard, butter, margarine and products like jam which were rich in sugar. Ration cards were issued showing how much each person was allowed to buy of each rationed item. The shopkeeper crossed each item off after the sale. Rationing

FANY ambulance driver (© Imperial War Museum)

made sure that nobody starved and gave a measure of fairness to the food supply situation. Nevertheless, a flourishing black market existed and wealthier people could buy a little extra for a lot extra. Country people could usually lay their hands on a turnip or two, a few eggs, some potatoes or a rabbit.

Britain's Prime Minister recalled the effects of rationing:

> "The steady improvement in our national health figures ... shows that compulsory temperance in eating was in general more beneficial than harmful in its effects. Although there was a degree of scarcity we were never faced with famine ..."
>
> (*War Memoirs of David Lloyd George*, page 795)

People ate more fibre and less fat and sugar. Nobody needed to diet.

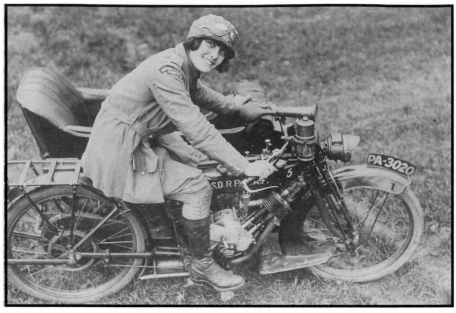

WRAF on a motor bike (© Imperial War Museum)

In Germany rationing was also introduced but the situation was much worse. Germany had been almost self-sufficient in food before the war, but food production fell when most of the men were called up to the army. Britain's Royal Navy imposed a tight blockade on German ports and prevented food imports. In the winter of 1917–18 over 500,000 German civilians died of starvation in what came to be known as the 'turnip winter' after the only form of food available.

WAACs tended the graves of fallen soldiers (© Imperial War Museum)

WOMEN AND THE WAR

The First World War was not an equal opportunities war, but there were many interesting and useful things for girls to do. When it broke out, a gigantic battle of the sexes was raging in Britain as the Suffragettes campaigned vigorously and violently for the right for women to vote, although it has to be said that battle lines were not drawn strictly along gender lines. Mrs Pankhurst, the Suffragette leader, quickly called off the campaign and urged women to do all they could to help the war effort. The government, however, was slow to make use of women and in July 1917 Mrs Pankhurst organised a huge procession of women through London. This was later known as 'the right to serve march'.

When Dr Elsie Inglis offered the British government a one hundred bed medical unit staffed

Above: Women were employed in engineering shops which were the sole preserve of men prior to the war. Here they are employed in producing Howitzers.

Below: Women filling machine gun belts (© Imperial War Museum)

The Women's Forestry Corps (© Imperial War Museum)

entirely by Scottish women (ambulance drivers, nurses and doctors) it was suggested that they would be better employed knitting socks. Dr Inglis had been involved in the campaign for women to be allowed to train as doctors and had been among the first women to qualify in medicine in Scotland. A prominent campaigner for the right to vote for women, she did not readily take 'no' for an answer. Her medical unit was accepted by the French and was based at Royaumont Abbey. It rapidly expanded to six hundred beds and was recognised as one of the most efficient hospitals in France. Inglis, herself, set up another medical unit which went to Serbia where she died, due to the hardship of war, in 1917. A Serb general said, "We would rather have lost a battle than lose her." The maternity hospital, which she had established in Edinburgh, bore her name as a memorial from 1923 until its closure in 1988.

Slowly the government came to realise that the war would not be won unless all human resources were utilised to the full, and those included women and girls.

Women in the Services

About 25,000 women went to the front but will nevertheless be dealt with here in a chapter on the home front! The armed forces had, in fact, employed women before the war. In 1902 Queen Alexandra's Imperial Military Nursing Service had been set up, but it numbered only three hundred nurses when the war broke out. Thousands more were quickly recruited from the Service's own reserve and from civilian hospitals. There were not nearly enough professional nurses to cope with the huge number of casualties so the VAD (Voluntary Aid Detachment) was created from young women with no previous nursing experience. Typical of these was Vera

Brittain who was in her first year at Oxford University when the war broke out. By the end of the war her brother, her boyfriend and most of her male acquaintances had been killed or maimed. Vera's war was spent in makeshift hospitals nursing men with horrific injuries, often listening to them groaning until they died. In the end she exhibited most of the symptoms of men traumatised by battle—depression, anger, compulsion to talk about her experiences, bad dreams. Like all VADs, she learned the skills of nursing on the job. Many of these girls staffed the huge tented hospitals which the army created a few miles behind the lines. In winter duckboards were laid, but soon the nurses were struggling through a sea of mud to tend to their patients. Although these hospitals were clearly marked with large red cross signs they were hit, not infrequently, by enemy shells and bombs, killing patients, nurses and doctors alike. There were those who believed that they were deliberately targeted.

The First Aid Nursing Yeomanry (FANY) was created in 1907 to give battlefield first aid, but their role changed to that of driving ambulances and army transport, the first women to drive for the services. This much decorated service was the only women's organisation not to be disbanded at the end of the war.

By working as cooks or drivers in Queen Mary's Army Auxiliary Corps women freed men for fighting service. By the end of the war there were 57,000 of them.

The other services were a little slow to copy the army's example, but in 1917 the Women's Royal Naval Service ('Wrens') was created and women were given shore work to do, including the vitally important task of sending shore to ship radio signals. There were 7,000 Wrens when the war ended. Women also became wireless operators, drivers, typists, telephonists and storekeepers in the new Wom-en's Royal Air Force, set up in 1918. Some were trained to service the aircraft. The WRAF had a strength of 32,000 when hostilities ceased.

Women in Manufacturing Industry

In the early stages of the war Britain quickly experienced a crisis with ammunition supplies. The army fired off shells and bullets much faster than industry could produce them. In May 1915 David Lloyd George was put in charge of the new Ministry of Munitions. A politician with a sharp mind and a capacity for original ideas, Lloyd George was quick to exploit female labour in the munitions factories. Initially this was purely 'a man's job' but by late 1918, 90% of the workers were women. Girls who could have earned 25p per week as domestic servants were tempted by wages of £4 a week—but there was often a price. Lloyd George recorded in his memoirs that trouble had been experienced with shell detonators, bought in America, unscrewing in flight with the result that the shell did not explode on impact.

"To prevent this the screwed-in gaines had to be stabbed in two places with cold chisel and hammer to break the thread so that they would not unscrew.

Women workers in the factory at Hayes undertook a large part of this … risky work, for if a fulminate were ignited by the blow, the gaine would explode and disembowel them. One morning news came in that there had been a terrible explosion at Hayes, in which several women had been killed. My representative went to visit the scene. Work was being done in a number of little huts … . One of them was badly shattered. At its entrance Lord Lee ran against a busy little woman, about five feet high, white faced but resolute. 'Is this where the explosion took place?' he asked. 'Yes,' she answered. … He saw bloodstains on the floor and the survivors carrying on at full speed with hammer and cold chisel. Lord Lee spoke with the little forewoman. When the explosion had occurred that morning she had calmed and steadied her girls and headed them back to their grim and dangerous task. All she would say was: 'I am not going to run

Numbers of Women in Paid Employment

Sector	July 1914	July 1918	% change
Self-employed & employers	430,000	470,000	+9.3
Industry	2,178,600	2,970,600	+36.3
Domestic Service	1,658,000	1,258,000	-24.1
Commerce	505,500	934,500	+84.9
National & Local government (including teaching)	262,200	460,200	+75.5
Agriculture	190,000	228,000	+20.0
Hotels, public houses, theatres	181,000	220,000	+21.5
Transport	18,200	117,200	+643.6
Other Professions	542,500	652,000	+20.2
Totals	5,966,000	7,310,500	+22.5

Table 6.1 (Source Gill Thomas, *Women in the First World War* in *Hindsight* magazine September 1990)

away, especially when I think about those poor boys in France who are facing more dangers than we are.' "
(*War Memoirs of David Lloyd George* page 353)

When the Vanesta Works in East London blew up in January 1917, sixty nine people were killed outright, about 1,000 were injured and hundreds were made homeless. In all, two hundred and thirty seven were killed in such explosions. One hundred and four women died of TNT poisoning.

Later Lloyd George wrote:

"The courage of the girls and women engaged in these factories has never been sufficiently recognised. They had to work under conditions of real danger to life and limb, and what some of them probably dreaded still more, of grotesque disfigurement—for one of the perils … (of) the shell filling factories was toxic jaundice resulting from TNT poisoning. This ailment turned their faces a bright and repulsive yellow. The poor girls … were nicknamed …'canaries.' They were quite proud of this designation, for they had earned it in the path of duty."
(*War Memoirs of David Lloyd George* page 352)

Agriculture

The crisis caused by the second U-boat campaign led to the creation of the Women's Land Army in 1917. Many of those who served were city girls from middle-class homes, quite unaccustomed to hard physical labour. Few failed to impress the initially doubtful farmers with their grit and determination. In the end they helped to save the country from starvation. Other women joined the Forestry Corps and felled the trees needed in the shipbuilding and other industries.

Glasgow tram conductress. Glasgow was quick to utilise female labour.
(© Imperial War Museum)

Transport

At the start of the war almost the entire staff of the Glasgow Corporation Tramways Department left to form a special battalion of the Highland Light Infantry. Glasgow got its first female clippies in April 1915, followed more slowly by Manchester and London. Women also became bus drivers and greasers on the railways.

Counter Espionage

Concern about German spies led to the creation of MI5 (Military Intelligence, Department 5) shortly before the war. Women clerical staff kept records of agents' reports. During the war they used Boy Scouts to run errands and transfer files between sections, but the boys proved to be unreliable and were replaced by Girl Guides who were much more satisfactory. It is not recorded whether anybody went so far, then, as to say the future is female.

Outcome

The Duke of Wellington said that the Battle of Waterloo (1815) was a "damn close-run thing"; so was the 'Great War'. Without the huge contribution made by women, Britain would have undoubtedly ended up on the losing side. This gave the government the opportunity to back down on the issue of voting rights. In June 1918, before the war was over, *The Representation of the People Act* gave the right to vote to women over thirty who were householders, wives of householders or were university graduates. They had to wait another ten years, until 1928, before they were enfranchised on an equal basis with men at the age of twenty one.

When the war was over, most women left, or were forced to leave, the paid employment they had taken. Despite this the war brought significant changes to their lives. They began to wear trousers, to smoke in public and respectable young women might now go out with a young man, unaccompanied by

Recruits queuing at a London recruiting office early in the war (© Imperial War Museum)

a chaperon. After the Second World War their daughters would be much more reluctant to give up their jobs.

RECRUITMENT

When the war began there was mass enthusiasm for it all over Europe as hundreds of thousands of men and boys rushed to join up. In Britain 900,000 volunteered in the first three months. Lord Kitchener, Britain's most famous general, had been put in charge of recruitment with a target of 100,000 men in six months. 500,000 enlisted in August alone, but some were younger than the eighteen years of age they claimed to be and lads as young as fifteen later died for King and Country. Britain had not been involved in a big war for over fifty years and men had forgotten what war

was like. Many were bored by humdrum jobs, poverty or unemployment and looked for a little excitement. Lads who had lived their lives in dreadful industrial cities saw it as a chance to visit France, taste French wine, meet French girls, come back a hero in uniform and make a big impression on the girls back home. Sadly it did not work out like that. They were also terrified that it would "all be over by Christmas" and they would miss all the action.

Those more reluctant to volunteer found themselves the victims of psychological pressure. Recruitment posters played on traditional ideas of manhood and urged men to defend their women from the 'beastly Hun' and women to reject men not in uniform as unworthy of their af-

fection. White feathers, "symbols of cowardice" were pinned on men in civilian clothes by patriotic ladies.

As the months and years passed it became clear that the war was not an exciting and glamorous adventure. As a trail of mutilated men returned home, some to die, the flood of volunteers dropped to a trickle. On an average sort of day about five hundred British servicemen would be killed and many more badly wounded. They had to be replaced.

In January 1916 Parliament passed the *Military Service Act* under which unmarried men aged eighteen to forty one were conscripted into the armed forces—they were forced to join. In May 1916 conscription was extended to married men of the same ages and in April 1918 the upper age limit was raised to fifty one. All the major powers of Europe, such as France and Germany, routinely conscripted men into their forces, even in peacetime, but for Britain conscription was new and was viewed by some as a serious breach of the indidual's rights.

Men could be excused service on the grounds of:

➡ being engaged in vital war work such as coal mining, shipbuilding or farming;

➡ being weak or in ill health;

➡ having dependents, such as an old widowed mother;

➡ objecting on grounds of conscience to fighting and killing.

The last clause was most unusual in Europe and straight away about 16,500 men objected. These can be split, broadly, into three groups.

1 *Religious objectors*—These tended to be guided by the Old Testament commandment "Thou shalt not kill". Prominent among these were members of the Society of Friends, or Quakers, whose absolute opposition to violence and war had been known for 300 years.

Conscientious Objectors in Britain, 1916

Likely total	16,500
Appearing before tribunals	14,000
Granted absolute exemption	400
Granted conditional exemption	6,000
Ordered to do non-combatant duty	5,000
Case rejected – Ordered to enlist	2,500
Objectors refusing to obey tribunal	6,000

Table 6.2 (Source: *Conscientious Objectors 1916 to the Present Day*. Tressell Publications 1988.)

2 *Political objectors*—Most of these were socialists. They believed that a German worker was the class brother of a British worker and that it was wrong for one to kill the other in what was a war started by capitalists, or bosses. Many had believed, before it began, that war was impossible as the workers would refuse to fight each other. James Keir Hardie, founder of the Labour Party, was a prominent anti-war campaigner while Fenner Brockway, later a long-serving Labour MP, was a conscientious objector, or 'conchie'.

3 *Pacifists*—These were people who simply believed that war was wrong. The term could be applied to the Quakers and the socialists as well as to those who, for no religious or political reason, felt that the war would be impossible if men refused to fight.

No European power, other than Britain, allowed men to avoid conscription on the grounds of conscience. Special Tribunals were set up to hear the cases of objectors. These were not like ordinary courts. An army officer would question the objector and a panel of well-known people from the area would hear the arguments. The panel might include landowners, businessmen, councillors, farmers, solicitors etc. They would have been urged by the government to get as many men as possible for the army. Four decisions were possible.

➤ *Absolute exemption*: The objector was excused all military duty.

➤ *Conditional exemption*: The objector did not have to enlist but had to do other work of national importance, such as working on the land or in forests.

➤ *Exemption from Combat*: The objector would have to join the army but would be given a non-fighting role, such as stretcher bearer.

➤ *Rejection*: The objector was ordered to join the army.

The tribunal specialised in difficult or trick questions. An objector would be asked: "What would you do if you came home and found a large and hairy Hun assaulting your mother or sister?" If the reply suggested any form of force or violence the man would be told: "If you are willing to use force to defend your family you should be willing to use it to defend your country."

Those who refused to enlist in the army became subject to military discipline. Some were sentenced to death for refusing orders although the sentence was always reduced if the 'conchie' still refused to give in. Many refused non-combatant duty on the grounds that it simply released another man to kill. Special prisons and work camps were opened up to supplement the ordinary prisons to which many objectors were sent. Twenty four died while detained at Home Office work centres.

In the community, conscientious objectors were often subjected to a torrent of verbal and sometimes physical abuse. Milder forms of this treatment included being ignored and being refused service in shops. Serving soldiers, home on leave from the trenches, often seemed strangely reluctant to take part in the 'conchie baiting'.

PROPAGANDA
Somebody once said that the first casualty of war is truth. During the war, civilian

RED CROSS OR IRON CROSS?

WOUNDED AND A PRISONER
OUR SOLDIER CRIES FOR WATER.
THE GERMAN "SISTER"
POURS IT ON THE GROUND BEFORE HIS EYES.
THERE IS NO WOMAN IN BRITAIN
WHO WOULD DO IT.
THERE IS NO WOMAN IN BRITAIN
WHO WILL FORGET IT.

We risk our lives to bring you food.
It's up to you not to
waste it.

REMEMBER BELGIUM

ENLIST TO-DAY

BRITISH PROPAGANDA
POSTERS

THE ZEPPELIN RAIDS: THE VOW OF VENGEANCE
Drawn for 'The Daily Chronicle' by Frank Brangwyn ARA

'DAILY CHRONICLE' READERS ARE
COVERED AGAINST THE RISKS OF
BOMBARDMENT BY ZEPPELIN OR
AEROPLANE

populations were constantly bombarded with propaganda.

Propaganda consists of claims issued by a government, political party or other organisation, presented as news or information, in which the truth is twisted, distorted or ignored. Propaganda is often designed to appeal to people's emotions rather than to reason.

Much of the British government's propaganda was fairly mild stuff designed to persuade people to black out the windows of their houses so that German airmen could not see the lights, or not to waste food. Some of the material in recruiting posters or directed against the Germans was of a stronger brew. Consider the following account of events in Belgium early in the war.

"Reports of German atrocities fanned the flame of moral indignation and oddly the Germans were responsible for all but the most lurid ... They were quick to realise the advantages of allowing foreign journalists to put the German case in neutral countries, especially America. Neutral correspondents were welcome to follow the German army ...

'Frightfulness' was the Germans' own word ... If the Germans were to advance quickly then the civil population must be smartly brought to heel and harsh measures against francs, tireurs, saboteurs and those who harboured enemy soldiers were calculated to spread terror ... (so that) only a minimal number of troops would be needed to garrison a town. As soon as a district was occupied, hostages would be taken ... If a single German was molested or injured the hostages would be shot.

(Terrified Belgian refugees carried stories to Britain which were confirmed by American journalists.)

There were first-hand accounts from people who had escaped from the flames of Andenne where 200 hostages were shot, from Tamines, where 400 were gunned down, and from the inhabitants of Dinant who had annoyed the Germans by destroying a vital bridge. The Germans' revenge was to round up more than 600 men, women and children and to shoot them in cold blood. The youngest, aged three weeks, died in his mother's arms. The stories were true and the Germans made no attempt to keep them secret. They were, after all, intended to warn. Inevitably, as they travelled, they spawned fictions in their wake—of rape, of macabre killings, of mutilation, of breasts and hands sliced off by sabres, of crucifixions, of babies dipped in boiling water or swung for sport against brick walls. There were even whispers of cannibalism."
(Lynn MacDonald, *1914* pages 210–213)

Few items of propaganda went as far as the story of the corpse recycling plant.

"I feel I must mention a piece of psychological propaganda, put about by some war office person, which brought poor comfort to Tommies. The story swept the world and, being gullible, we in the trenches were taken in by it for a while. With slight variations it indicated that the German war industry was in a bad way, and was short of fats for making glycerine. To overcome the shortage a vast secret factory had been erected in the Black Forest, to which the bodies of British soldiers were dispatched. The bodies, wired together in bundles, were pitchforked onto conveyor belts and moved into the factory for conversion into fats. War artists and cartoonists got busy, and dreadful scenes were depicted and published in Britain."
(George Coppard, *With a Machine Gun to Cambrai* page 116)

OTHER RESTRICTIONS ON CIVILIANS

On 8 August 1914, after the briefest of debates, Parliament passed *The Defence of the Realm Act* (DORA) which placed numerous restrictions on ordinary citizens. Many of these were remarkable even in wartime, few would have been tolerated in peacetime and some seem downright trivial.

It was forbidden to

✗ Give bread to dogs, poultry, horses or other animals.
✗ Buy an alcoholic drink for somebody else, unless as a dinner host.
✗ Buy binoculars without official permission.
✗ Melt down gold or silver.
✗ Fly a kite which could be used for signalling.
✗ Send a letter abroad written, wholly or partly, in invisible ink.
✗ Talk about naval or military affairs in public.

This act gave the military authorities the power to arrest civilians and try them in courts martial (army courts) for a wide range of offences such as those listed above. Some of the provisions, however, were less trivial.

● Railways and dockyards came under military law.

● Censorship was introduced. Newspapers were not allowed to give details of battles where things had gone badly wrong for Britain. Heavy casualty figures were played down and few facts emerged about German air raids on Britain. At Etaples, on the French coast, the British army had a massive training camp where both men coming out of the trenches and new recruits were subjected to a regime of physical abuse, bullying and humiliation by instructors and the Military Police. In 1917 their patience finally snapped. Aubrey Aaransan of the Border Regiment later recalled:

> "It was one hell of a riot that went on for nights and days. Some drunken soldiers broke into the WAAC billets and chased the girls through the streets. Later word came down from Toplis (ringleader), 'Stop chasing the girls, get the Military Police instead'. His orders were obeyed. I remember six military policemen, shot during the riots, being buried in one grave ... outside Etaples. Mutineers flocked to the grave side to sing bawdy, comical songs. They roared down a padrc's attempt to put up a prayer for the dead policemen."
>
> (William Allison and John Fairly, *The Monocled Mutineer* page 109)

Press censorship ensured that neither the British public nor the Germans ever read about this massive, self-imposed, crisis in the British army. Furthermore, they never read about the multiple rapes of women serving with the WAAC near Etaples, nor of the numerous executions by firing squad after the event. The colonies of deserters hiding out in the caves and sand dunes along the coast were also kept secret. The cover-up was highly effective. Charles Miller, on officer who witnessed the events said:

> "What did intrigue me about the mutiny was the way it was hushed up. I have never seen a whisper of it in any book about the war."
>
> (William Allison and John Fairly, *The Monocled Mutineer*)

The silence was only broken sixty one years later with the publication of *The Monocled Mutineer* in 1978 and by the TV programme of the same name in 1986.

Source

May 26 1917   The Scots Pictorial

ONE WOMAN TO ANOTHER
By "M. B."

The Flapper Type

The war, it would appear, has not had a spiritualising effect on some women, very much the reverse. Of the majority this cannot be said, thank heavens, but the war is responsible for the appearance of an especially obnoxious kind of flapper—soulless, greedy, immodest—who infests all streets of all towns where men in uniform congregate. She does not mean any harm, I take it; she is out for 'a bit of fun' ... but she is living a life that does not improve young girlhood, and she is providing soldiers from overseas with a wrong idea of the women of Britain.

The Forgetful Wife

Again there is the young woman whom the war has separated from her husband. One would think that the fact that she is left to keep the flag of the home flying while her husband is enduring the hell of the trenches would have a steadying effect on the most frivolous, but among the wives of the humbler class this is not always so ... Public houses are full of women, some of whom, hitherto respectable, are now associating with others who have lost all self-respect ... Nor do I find that the woman who forgets her husband, her children and her sense of decency is confined to one class and that the lowest. The wives of not a few officers have taken advantage of their emancipation to go to extremes that they would never have landed in if they had been living under the care of their spouses.

In the main our women are all right, and more than all right; the bravest of the brave, the most patient of the patient, the most noble in a time when the ordinary man has to discover bravery and courage ... to carry him through life.

(From *The Scots Pictorial* 26 May 1917)

Later, the *Munitions Act* made it illegal for workers in industries important to the war effort, such as shipbuilding, to go on strike. This did not stop a number of strikes on Clydeside between 1915 and the end of the war by shipyard engineers, who feared that they would be replaced by women and American machine tools and sent off to the front. They saw that their bosses wanted to use the war as an excuse to crush trade union strength.

DORA also forbade men in vital industries, such as coal mining, to leave their job or join the army. At the same time workers in unimportant jobs could be redirected to where they could do more for the war effort.

Dictators such as Hitler and Mussolini have often been condemned for similar interferences with the freedom of the individual. Is a democratic state, like Britain, justified in imposing such measures in wartime?

The Cost of the War

It has been estimated that the Great War cost £74,859,218,000. Of this £14,912,000,000 represents the cash value of the soldiers who died. This figure was reached by calculating how much they would have earned in the rest of their lives if they had not been killed. It places a value of about £1,500 on each man who died, which might seem reasonably generous when one considers that many men in Britain at that time were paid little more than £1 per week.

When the war broke out the British army had to reject many volunteers on the grounds that they were physically unfit to die for their country. Emerging from their slums, keen to serve King and Country, they were found to be undersized, flat of foot, wrecked by rickets and to have terrible teeth. In short they suffered from every possible consequence of bad diet and the army had to reduce its minimum height requirement from 5 feet 4 inches to 5 feet to allow the wee men from Glasgow to serve in a special bantams bat-

talion. Yet a country which seemed unable to feed, house and offer decent medical treatment to over a quarter of its people was able to spend £7,852,000,000 on a war.

In economic terms, the war was very costly for Britain. During the war she was forced to neglect her export trade and lost crucial markets in South America and the Far East to the USA and Japan. These markets were never really recovered. Although she lent money to her allies, she borrowed heavily her-

Many victims of the war lost limbs. These men were at Roehampton hospital (© The Imperial War Museum)

self from America and ended the war with a hugely increased national debt and her gold reserves (savings) wiped out.

Most estimates put the military deaths for all countries at about nine million. These were equalled by civilian deaths, roughly half of which can be attributed to starvation and disease and half to the massacre of Armenians, Greeks, Jews and Syrians by the Turks. The war left the world's population severely weakened due to malnutrition and contributed to the huge toll of deaths in the Spanish influenza epidemic which followed, claiming perhaps 20,000,000 lives worldwide—more than the war itself.

Scotland bore a heavy cost:

"Ludendorff said that the Scottish Divisions were the best divisions on the Western Front … They were good soldiers but there was a price, a price that makes you think. There were half a million Scots in the war but 115,000 of them were killed, one in every four of the Scots in France. Proportionately twice as many Scots were killed by comparison to all other units of the Empire's army … The generals

G v R I

HE whom this scroll commemorates was numbered among those who, at the call of King and Country, left all that was dear to them, endured hardness, faced danger, and finally passed out of the sight of men by the path of duty and self-sacrifice, giving up their own lives that others might live in freedom. Let those who come after see to it that his name be not forgotten.

Pioneer James Duncan Kennedy Robertson Royal Engineers

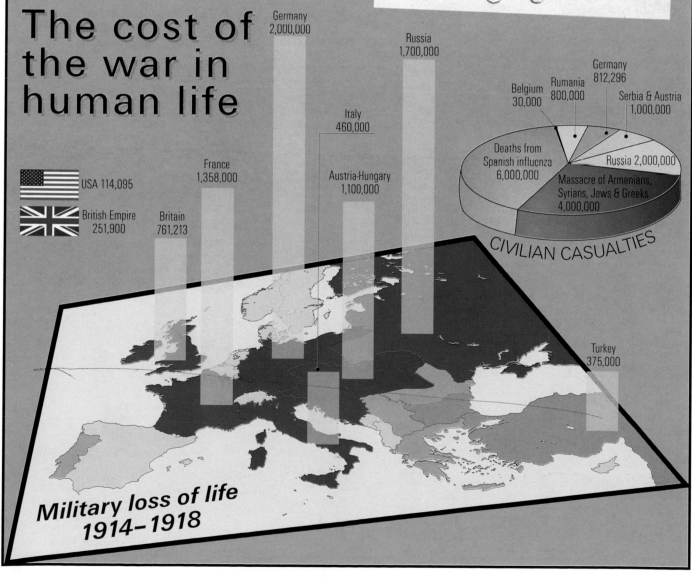

The cost of the war in human life

USA 114,095

British Empire 251,900

Britain 761,213

France 1,358,000

Germany 2,000,000

Russia 1,700,000

Italy 460,000

Austria-Hungary 1,100,000

Turkey 375,000

Military loss of life 1914–1918

CIVILIAN CASUALTIES

Belgium 30,000

Rumania 800,000

Germany 812,296

Serbia & Austria 1,000,000

Deaths from Spanish influenza 6,000,000

Russia 2,000,000

Massacre of Armenians, Syrians, Jews & Greeks 4,000,000

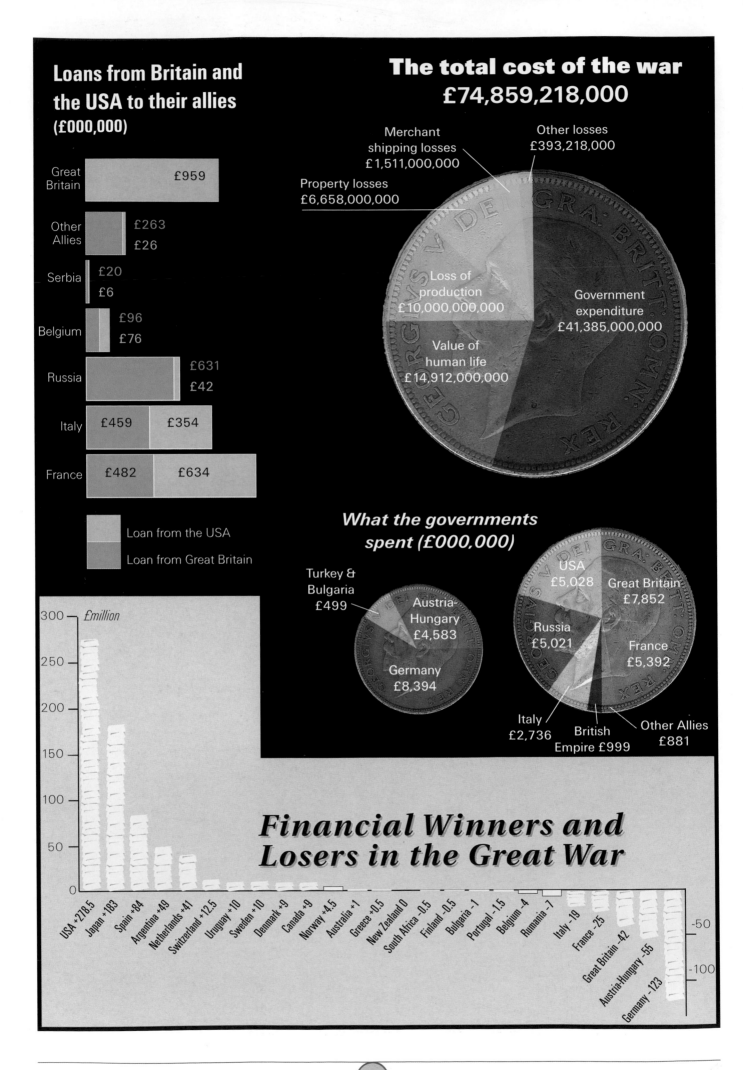

Loans from Britain and the USA to their allies
(£000,000)

Great Britain	£959
Other Allies	£263 / £26
Serbia	£20 / £6
Belgium	£96 / £76
Russia	£631 / £42
Italy	£459 / £354
France	£482 / £634

Loan from the USA
Loan from Great Britain

The total cost of the war
£74,859,218,000

Merchant shipping losses £1,511,000,000

Other losses £393,218,000

Property losses £6,658,000,000

Loss of production £10,000,000,000

Government expenditure £41,385,000,000

Value of human life £14,912,000,000

What the governments spent (£000,000)

Turkey & Bulgaria £499

Austria-Hungary £4,583

Germany £8,394

USA £5,028

Great Britain £7,852

Russia £5,021

France £5,392

Italy £2,736

British Empire £999

Other Allies £881

Financial Winners and Losers in the Great War

£million

300
250
200
150
100
50
0
-50
-100

USA +278.5, Japan +183, Spain +84, Argentina +49, Netherlands +41, Switzerland +12.5, Uruguay +10, Sweden +10, Denmark +9, Canada +9, Norway +4.5, Australia +1, Greece -0.5, New Zealand 0, South Africa -0.5, Finland -0.5, Bulgaria -1, Portugal -1.5, Belgium -4, Rumania -7, Italy -19, France -25, Great Britain -42, Austria-Hungary -55, Germany -123

knew they were good and put them in hard, difficult places."
[Donald MacCormack in conversation with Florrie Maclean on BBC Radio nan Gaidheal (translated)]

The Scottish National War Memorial in Edinburgh Castle has records of 148,151 Scots who died in the war, but this figure includes Scots serving in English regiments, in the Navy, and also those in Canadian, Australian and New Zealand units. Over 240,000 British servicemen had at least one arm or leg amputated as a result of the war.

At the start of the war it was common for men from one area or organisation all to join one unit of the army, forming 'Pals Battalions'. Thus emerged the Artists Rifles, the Church Lads, the Northern Cyclists Battalion and the Accrington Pals. Hearts seemed set to win the 1914–15 League when the entire team joined up en masse, the only professional football team in Britain to do so. Within a week,

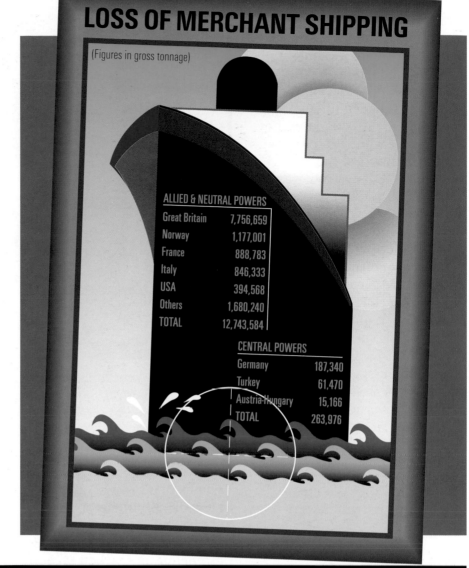

LOSS OF MERCHANT SHIPPING

(Figures in gross tonnage)

ALLIED & NEUTRAL POWERS

Great Britain	7,756,659
Norway	1,177,001
France	888,783
Italy	846,333
USA	394,568
Others	1,680,240
TOTAL	12,743,584

CENTRAL POWERS

Germany	187,340
Turkey	61,470
Austria-Hungary	15,166
TOTAL	263,976

La Targette—the French military cemetary near Vimy Ridge. Only one-third of the graves are shown here.

four hundred Tynecastle season ticket holders had joined up and by the end of a fortnight 1,350 fans had followed their team into Khaki. Seven men out of the squad of fifteen were to die. The 16th Battalion of the Royal Scots, which also contained members of the Watsonians Rugby Club, was known as the Edinburgh Sportsmen's Battalion.

Pals Battalions worked well until a major offensive which could widow every young mother in a community. One hundred men out of 850 in the 5th Camerons survived the Battle of Loos in 1915. This was a purely Gaelic-speaking Battalion drawn from the islands and mainland Inverness-shire. Loos was a devastating blow to many an already fragile Highland community and to their distinctive culture.

The financial costs and the death toll are reasonably easy to calculate. No figures can be put on the physical pain and emotional suffering which the war produced. Remarque dedicated *All Quiet on the Western Front* to "... a generation of men who, even though they may have escaped its shells, were destroyed by the war."

All veterans found it hard to adjust to civilian life again as life had become meaningless. More than the day they dreaded the night and the dreams which took them back.

On the British memorials to the missing—those with no known grave—there are 54,896 names

The Menin Gate in Ypres was built as a memorial to British soldiers killed in the salient up to August 1917 and who have no known grave. It bears the names of 54,896 men. Dedicated in 1927, it stands on the site of the old Menin Gate through which many soldiers passed on their way to the front and death.

on the Menin Gate in Ypres, 34,888 more in nearby Tyne Cott Cemetery and 73,412 on the Thiepval Monument on the Somme. It is immensely difficult to come to terms with the death of someone close when no body is ever found and no grave site known.

"We were on a working party ... when my chum Ernie Gayes got killed. We were working at night in the dark and there was shelling all the time and machine gun fire. It was a machine gun bullet that got Ernie. It was the worst job I had to do in the whole war—was to bury my own pal. People at home they had no idea what it was like; you didn't tell them. I wrote to Ernie's mother after he was killed ... just to tell her we'd buried him decently ..."
(Corporal J Smith, Northern Cyclists Battalion on *Gone for a Soldier* STV 1988)

Ernie was buried during heavy shell fire. One of his friends said: "I don't suppose he'd be there very long."

"I was only 5 when he was killed ... My mother never believed ... never really believed that Ernie had died. Years later we'd be in the town, walking through the market, and she'd clutch your arm and say, 'I'm sure I saw Ernie over there!' "
(Ethel Gayes on *Gone for a Soldier* STV 1988)

Eighty years after it ended old men wept as they placed poppies on the memorials to their fallen comrades in France and Flanders.

"You didn't tell them what it was like. They'd never understand. How could they?"

Nor can the true cost ever be calculated.

The End of the War

In April 1917 the USA declared war on Germany. The most important reason for this was American anger at U-boat attacks on merchant and neutral shipping which, over the years, had caused the death of hundreds of US citizens. The pressure was then on Germany to win quickly before the huge industrial and human resources of 'Uncle Sam' could be brought to bear on the Western Front. The Americans, however, were slow to get troops on the ground, insisting that they should be thoroughly trained and equipped before setting foot on the fields of carnage.

The Russian Czar had been deposed in a revolution in March 1917. Russia tried to fight on, but the hardship caused by the war led to a second, Communist, revolution in November of that year. Lenin came to power with the slogan 'Peace! Bread! Land!' and Russia was effectively out of the war. In April 1918 the Russians were forced to sign the harsh and humiliating treaty of Brest-Litovsk, handing over huge areas of Russia's best farmland to Germany. The collapse of Russia enabled large numbers of German and Austro-Hungarian troops to be transferred to the Western

Front. In the Spring of 1918 the Germans under General Ludendorff launched a series of desperate offensives against first the British and then the French.

KIRSTY WARK (NARRATOR): For four months it appeared that the German commander, Ludendorff, was achieving what Haig could not, a dramatic offensive victory.

PROFESSOR TREVOR WILSON: Ludendorff produces striking success and gets his army forward forty miles and by the time he has advanced forty miles he has outrun his artillery and is naked to his en-

The mule track by Paul Nash (© *Imperial War Museum*)

emies and is suffering prohibitive casualties.

KIRSTY WARK (NARRATOR): During that period the German army suffered almost one million dead and wounded; more than double the number of casualties suffered by the British in the Somme offensive of 1916.
(From BBC TV *TimeWatch* on Haig)

The Ludendorff offensive highlighted the fact that discipline was breaking down in the Kaiser's army. Half-starved soldiers stopped fighting to loot French homes for food and wine. One account tells of a mass of drunk Germans staggering down a road towards a concealed British machine gun. No prisoners were taken.

The Allies then began systematically to roll back the enemy using the painful lessons learned on the Somme and at Passchendaele. First the artillery totally pulverised a small section of the German trenches. Infantry, supported by tanks and aircraft, moved up under a creeping barrage[1] to take possession of the shattered ground, but did not attempt to advance again until the artillery had moved forward and neutralised the next line of defence.

8 August 1918 was the 'Black Day of the German Army'. Ludendorff wrote in his memoirs:

"whole bodies of our men surrendered to single troopers, or isolated squadrons. Retiring troops meeting fresh divisions going bravely into action had shouted things like 'Black-leg' and 'You're prolonging the war' … 400,000 prisoners were taken and more than 7,000 artillery pieces were captured, but some of the old problems remained. Of 415 tanks which attacked at Amiens, only 145 were left the next day."

In September, forty two British and two American divisions faced fifty seven German divisions holding the formidable Hindenburg Line.

"the position was for the most part covered in formidable water lines, deep canal-trenches impassable to tanks … protected in advance by acres of the densest barbed wire, arranged in great overlapping chequers … The artillery had to be called upon for a prolonged work of devastating fury … Altogether 25,000 tons of metal were discharged in a million shells. All battery positions, all headquarters, and all the entrances of the great tunnel-dugouts were deluged with a continuous rain of mustard gas … Early on the 27th British armies crossed the Canal du Nord against a half-dazed resistance … Their passage over the great canal at Bellenglise was a marvel of combined courage and organisation. They crossed with life-belts, rafts, and portable bridges in the teeth of machine-gun fire."
(CRMF Cruttwell, *A History of the Great War* pages 568 – 569)

It took only ten days to capture the Hindenburg line and gain access to the open country behind the trenches. The Germans tried to delay the allied advance by blowing up bridges and tearing up railway tracks.

"The damage done by Germany was immense, and little of it was made necessary by the dictates of war. In German occupied France nearly 300,000 houses were completely destroyed. Six thousand factories were stripped of their machin-ery which was sent to Germany. The textile mills of Lille and Sedan were smashed. Nearly 2,000 breweries were destroyed. In the coal mines round Roubaix and Tourcoing 112 shafts were blown in and 1,000 miles of underground galleries flooded or blocked. During their retreat the Germans burned and looted on a massive scale, destroying over 1,000 miles of railway line, blowing up 1,000 bridges, looting thousands of houses and stripping churches. During the four years of occupation the Germans took away half a million cows, half a million sheep, and over 300,000 horses and donkeys. These were the acts of vandals."
(Martin Gilbert writing in *Purnell's History of the 20th Century*, Chapter 32, pages 887–888)

Germany's allies began to capitulate. On 29 September Bulgaria surrendered, on 30 October the Turks gave up and on 3 November the Austro-Hungarian Empire collapsed as mutiny spread among its non-German troops such as the Poles, Slovaks and Czechs.

THE GERMAN REVOLUTION

The same process was at work among the war-weary people of Germany. In October a new civilian government was appointed in the hope that it would get the blame for defeat instead of the Kaiser and his army. On 29 October the fleet refused an order to put to sea for a last desperate attempt to beat the Royal Navy. Sailors mutinied and came ashore to join striking factory workers demanding peace. Copying the Communist revolution in Russia they set up workers' councils (Soviets) to run cities such as Kiel and Hamburg. On 9 November a general strike broke out. The government announced that the Kaiser had abdicated. He fled to Holland and

---

[1]*Creeping barrage*: An artillery technique gradually perfected during the war. Attacking troops began to advance while the artillery were still shelling the front line. As they drew close the artillery adjusted their range and began to drop shells on the next line of targets, thus forcing the enemy to keep their heads down until the attackers arrived. In its earliest form the creeping barrage was attempted by a series of timed 'lifts' of the artillery bombardment.

the government asked the Allies for an armistice.

Discussions were arranged. The Allies demanded
- the immediate evacuation of the invaded countries, Belgium, Luxembourg and France, including Alsace-Lorraine;
- the surrender of large quantities of weapons including 5,000 artillery pieces, 25,000 machine guns and 1,700 aeroplanes, all U-boats and most of the German surface fleet;
- 5,000 railway engines, 150,000 wagons and 5,000 lorries;
- that the Germans evacuate the left (west) bank of the Rhine which would then be occupied by allied troops;
- that the Germans agree to pay for the damage done in the war.

With the German army in a state of mutiny the new government had no alternative but to sign. On the 11th hour, of the 11th day of the 11th month 1918 the guns finally fell silent on the Western Front.

WHY DID GERMANY LOSE THE WAR?

The Failure of the Schlieffen Plan

Faced with a war on two fronts against a numerically superior enemy, the Triple Alliance had gambled on a quick victory. The Schlieffen plan failed to deliver this and Germany found herself facing a long war she was unlikely to win.

Failure of Alternative Strategies

When the Schlieffen plan failed,

Der Krieg by Otto Dix – *a German artist's view of the war*

the German High Command turned it on its head and tried to knock Russia out of the war while going on the defensive on the Western Front. They also tried to starve Britain out of the war with the U-boat campaigns. Russia was eventually destroyed, but not until the U-boat campaign had brought America into the war against Germany.

Naval Weakness

Despite the naval arms race, Germany failed to capture Britain's control of the sea. Germany's U-boat campaigns failed to starve Britain into submission, while Britain's surface fleet mounted a devastatingly effective blockade of Germany. Like a huge octopus the Royal Navy wrapped its tentacles round Germany and squeezed it to death, as it had done to Napoleon's France a century earlier.

Economic Failure

Despite its autocratic power, the Kaiser's government was less effective at organising all available resources for the war effort than democratic Britain. German agriculture failed to produce enough food and German industry could not supply the army with enough munitions.

Source

Our troops heard of the signing of the armistice at 10 a.m. this morning, which gave them an hour's more war, for the armistice came into force at 11 a.m. Without orders and without hesitation, every aeroplane loaded to the full with bombs, and flew off to give the retreating Hun a final dose, every gun belched forth rapid fire, using up every round of ammunition in the last hour of the Great War, every machine gun rattled out its last adieu and every man pressed forward regardless of risk, in his effort to have a last dig at the Hun in this his last hour of war. I understand that the Hun, on hearing that the armistice had been signed, abandoned fighting and was completely taken by surprise … It is said that he lost heavily from 10 to 11 a.m. this morning and completely failed to take his punishment in the spirit in which it was meant.

[Col. Richard Meinertzhagen, *Army Diary 1899–1926*
(Meinertzhagen, despite his German name, was an officer in the British army)]

Source

About 10.55 a.m. on Armistice Day, our artillery began to open fire on the Germans, and for five minutes every battery on the whole front was sending over salvo after salvo. The air was rent with the whining and shrieking of shells as they hurtled over our heads. All this of course sounded very much like permanent peace! However when 11 a.m. arrived the noise began to die down and comparative calm prevailed. I discovered later that the final five minutes of burst of fire was not due to any war-like spirit … but to the fact that every shell not used had to be carried back. The artillery … did not want to be bothered with live shells that would have to be carried, so they adopted the perfectly legitimate method of disposing of them in action. My utmost sympathy went out to the Germans … for many of them must have passed over to the Great Beyond in that final burst of fire.

(A Stuart Dolden, *Cannon Fodder*)

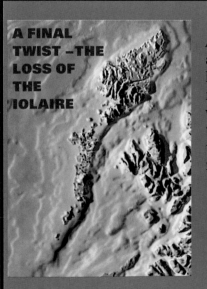
A FINAL TWIST – THE LOSS OF THE IOLAIRE

About 2.00 a.m. on New Year's Day 1919 the motor yacht, Iolaire, with a Royal Navy crew, ran into rocks and sank at the mouth of Stornoway harbour. Two hundred and five of the two hundred and eighty four men on board, mainly Lewis and Harris men returning from the war, were drowned. About eight hundred Lewis men had already died in the war. This final twist, when all seemed over, was almost too much to bear. It traumatised an island to the extent that for a generation or more nobody spoke of it.

"His father went on his knees beside him and began to take letters from his son's pockets, and there was money, I remember, silver and paper money, in the pockets of the trousers. And the father was reading a letter that he found and the tears were falling from him, splashing on the body of his son. I think it is the most heart-rending sight I have ever seen."
(Translation of Donald MacPhail speaking on a BBC Gaelic radio programme c 1959. Quoted in *Highlanders* by John MacLeod, page 302)

Versailles: Peacemaking 1919

THE PEACE CONFERENCE

The armistice was merely a cease-fire, not the end of the war. Before peace could be certain both sides would have to sign a peace treaty. While the terms of this treaty were being discussed, the Allies continued to blockade Germany and deny her food imports. German children continued to die of starvation.

Germany was finally presented with the terms of the Treaty in June 1919. It had been drawn up by a conference in the old French royal palace of Versailles, just a few miles southwest of Paris, a city seething with hate for everything German.

In the final stages of the war many countries declared war on Germany, just to be at the conference. No fewer than thirty two countries were represented at the discussions. Neutral nations, such as Sweden, who might have been able to offer reasonable, unbiased views, were not represented. The Russians were not present either. Although they had saved France in 1914 and had lost huge numbers of men in the war, they had committed the unforgivable sins of turning Communist and suing for peace. The defeated powers were not allowed to take part in, or even observe, the discussions. Towards the end they were permitted to make written comments on a draft copy of the Treaty. This led Hitler to describe it as the "Diktat of Versailles", a dictated treaty which he said Germany had been forced to sign and only needed to keep as long as she had no alternative. Most of the delegates had little influence on the proceedings. The majority of the decisions were taken by 'the Big Four', the leaders of the main allied countries.

France was represented by Georges Clemençeau, a fierce, cunning old man, who richly deserved his nickname, 'le tigre'. Twice in his lifetime he had seen the Germans invade and devastate his country. He was an old

The Menin Road by Paul Nash (© *Imperial War Museum*)

David Lloyd George, Britain's PM.

man of 79, in his twilight years, but life would yield one more pleasure. He would twist the knife in Germany's wound. He had four main aims, all of which begin with 'R'.

➤ Revenge on Germany for 1870 and for 1914–18.

➤ Ruin Germany so that it could never threaten France again.

➤ Restore Alsace and Lorraine to France.

➤ Reparations. Germany and her allies should pay for the total cost of the war and for the damage inflicted on France and Belgium.

David Lloyd George was Britain's Prime Minister. He listened carefully to advisers like the South African Boer, General Jan Smuts and the young diplomat, Harold Nicholson, who warned him of the dangers of a harsh peace which left Germany bitter and looking for revenge. He also knew that the British people wanted revenge on Germany almost as much as the French. Politicians demanded that they should "Squeeze the German lemon until the pips squeak." Lloyd George wanted a peace which would not be too hard on

Germany but at the same time he needed to convince the British voters that he had not agreed to a soft and easy peace. The British were also keen that Germany should be eliminated as a naval power.

Woodrow Wilson was the President of the USA. Although Wilson had been responsible for the racial segregation of the US civil service and a variety of other measures designed to reinforce the second-class citizenship of black Americans, he saw himself as the champion of democracy. He believed that democracy would solve Europe's problems and protect the world from European wars. In January 1918 he laid down fourteen points on which he believed peace should be based. These can be simplified to a number of basic principles. (See page 73)

Clemençeau remarked that God himself had been satisfied with ten commandments but that Wilson had fourteen. He also said "He talks like Jesus Christ and acts like Lloyd George." Some people had begun to see the British Prime Minister as a devious political trickster without guiding principles or morals.

The Germans expected the peace treaty to be based on the fourteen points. However, by the end of 1918 things had changed due to the harsh terms imposed on Russia by Germany and by much pointless destruction carried out in France by the retreating German armies.

Signor Orlando represented Italy and is often described as the fourth man in the 'big four'. He had little influence and was largely ignored by the other three. At one stage he left the conference and returned home in protest when Italy did not re-

ceive territory promised to her when she joined the Allies in 1915.

Each of the defeated countries signed a separate treaty, all of which were modelled on the German Treaty, the Treaty of Versailles. (See Table 9.1)

The peace settlement was a huge task which involved redrawing the map of Europe. The delegates found that they did not have enough time. Committees were set up to look at different parts. Each of these suggested the heaviest penalty which could be imposed on the defeated states, fully expecting the terms to be watered down. In the rush to draw up the treaty, Woodrow Wilson typed some of it himself on his portable typewriter. Only when the terms were presented to the Germans did anybody get an overall picture of the treaty. Just as some allied delegates, like the brilliant young Britons Harold Nicholson and John Maynard Keynes, began to criticise its severity, the Germans made the fatal mistake of releasing the details to their newspapers. The terms quickly became known round the world and it was impossible to change them without looking as if the allied leaders were being soft and giving in to the demands of the nasty Germans.

The Treaty was signed in the huge Hall of Mirrors where the new German Empire had been proclaimed forty eight years earlier. When all the allied delegates were seated Clemençeau said, "Bring in the Germans". Dr Muller and Dr Bell were ushered in, like criminals to a court. They signed and left by a side door. Those who feared that the Germans might refuse to sign altogether were most relieved.

WILSON'S FOURTEEN POINTS

1 An end to secret diplomacy. The terms of all treaties should be published to avoid the fear and insecurity caused by the growth of power blocks before the war.

2 Freedom of navigation on the high seas. In time of war as in peacetime the rights of neutral nations to trade anywhere should be respected. Warships should not stop and search neutral merchant ships.

3 Free Trade. Wilson was against all trade taxes, tariffs, and restrictions on trade.

4 Disarmament. All countries should greatly cut their armed forces, thus reversing the prewar arms race.

5 Germany should not be stripped of colonies and land by the Allies. Wilson spoke of a "just peace without annexations or indemnities."

6 Russia should be left in peace and not hounded for turning Communist.

7 Points 7 to 13 were concerned with the principle of Self-Determination. This was the idea that all peoples, races or nations had the right to govern themselves or decide how they would be governed. This implied that the map of Europe would be drastically changed. The Austro-Hungarian Empire would be split into its many component parts and Poland would emerge again as an independent nation after years of partition between Russia, Austria and Germany.

14 A League of Nations would be created to keep the peace. Countries would be encouraged to negotiate rather than fight, but the League could also take armed action against any unrepentant aggressor. Wilson got this idea from the South African general and statesman, Jan Smuts, but it became a matter of huge importance to him.

CRITICISMS OF THE TREATY

Nobody liked the Treaty. The French felt that it did not go far enough to protect them from German aggression. From the very beginning some British observers feared a treaty which would leave Germany bitter and thirsting for revenge. In 1923 David Lloyd George said:

> "You may strip Germany of her colonies, reduce her armaments to a mere police force and her navy to that of a fifth-rate power; all the same in the end if she feels that she has been unjustly treated in the Peace of 1919 she will find the means of exacting retribution from her conqueror."
> (quoted by Sarah Burnett in *Hindsight*, January 1991)

Some people felt that, while each part of the treaty could be justified, the package as a whole was too severe. Germany had lost all of her colonies, one-third of her coalfields, three-quarters of her iron ore fields and one-third of her blast furnaces and yet was still required to pay reparations after the means to make the money to pay the bill had been confiscated. Others felt that the peace settlement had neither been severe enough to crush Germany nor generous enough to give Europe a new beginning based on trust and friendship.

The Germans had many complaints. They resented the fact that they had not been allowed face-to-face negotiations. Hitler called the treaty a "diktat"—a dictated peace which Germany should reject as soon as she had the power to do so.

The war guilt clause was hated in a Germany where most people still believed the Kaiser's claim that Germany had been fighting a defensive war against encircling enemies, Russia and France. As a result of this the reparations clause was also hated and was seen as a way to destroy Germany.

The treaties with Austria and Germany left pockets of ethnic Germans scattered around Europe—800,000 of them in Po-

(continued on page 76)

COUNTRY	TREATY	SIGNING DATE
Germany	Versailles	28 June 1919
Austria	St Germain	10 September 1919
Bulgaria	Neuilly	27 November 1919
Hungary	The Trianon	4 June 1920
Turkey	Sevres	10 August 1920
Turkey (renegotiated)	Lausanne	24 July 1923

Table 9.1

EUROPE AFTER THE TREATY OF VERSAILLES

Figure 9.1

THE TERMS OF THE TREATY OF VERSAILLES

Territorial Terms

1 In Europe, Germany had to surrender the following:

➟ *to France* – Alsace and Lorraine. The Saar coalfield and its output would also go to France for fifteen years and then a plebiscite (referendum) would decide to which country this predominantly German region would belong.

➟ *to Belgium* – the small districts of Eupen and Malmedy.

➟ *to Denmark* – the border province of Schleswig after a plebiscite. This area had been taken by Prussia in 1864 and was overwhelmingly Danish speaking.

➟ *to the new state of Poland* – part of Upper Silesia, after a plebiscite, Posen and part of East Prussia. Poland was given a 'corridor to the sea' which left the remains of East Prussia isolated from the rest of Germany.

➟ *to the League of Nations* – the port of Danzig (now Gdansk) which was to be a free port available to both the Poles and the Germans of East Prussia. The territory of Memel between East Prussia and the new state of Lithuania also went to the League. Germany had to hand over the land taken from Russia in 1917. Some of this went to Poland, while Finland, Estonia, Latvia and Lithuania became independent. Russia lost more European territory by the peace settlement than any other power.

Delegates at Versailles. The Treaty was signed in the huge Hall of Mirrors where the new German Empire had been proclaimed forty eight years earlier.

Anschluss, union with Austria, was also forbidden. Since the Austrians are a German-speaking nation this led to claims that self-determination was for everyone—except the Germans.

2 Worldwide:
Germany was stripped of her colonial empire and the colonies handed over to the League of Nations. The League then divided them up among the victorious allies as 'mandated territories' which were to be ruled in the interest of their native peoples and prepared for independence as soon as possible. Germans were considered morally unsuitable to rule 'natives'.

Military and Naval Terms

1 The German army was restricted to 100,000 men. Conscription was forbidden and volunteers had to sign on for a minimum of twelve years.

2 Germany was forbidden to have any tanks or heavy artillery.

3 The General Staff (army planning branch) was to be disbanded and not re-formed.

4 Germany was not allowed to have an air force.

5 Germany was to hand her entire navy over to Britain. She would then be restricted to six small battleships of less than 10,000 tons—little more than half the size of a 'super-dreadnought' of 1918. She was to have no U-boats. (Under the armistice terms the German High Seas Fleet had surrendered to the British and was at anchor at Scapa Flow in the Orkneys. On hearing of the treaty terms the German crews scuttled their ships.)

6 The Rhineland, which remained part of Germany, was to be a demilitarised zone. Germany was to have no troops or fortifications between the French border and a line drawn 50 kilometres to the east of the River Rhine. This was to give France ample warning of any future invasion so that any war would be fought on German rather than on French soil.

Other terms

1 War Guilt: Germany had to accept responsibility for starting the war.

2 Reparations: Since Germany was considered to be guilty of having started the war, she had to pay for the cost of the war. No sum was fixed at the time but a Reparations Commission was set up to consider the matter. It quickly became obvious that the enemy could not pay for every bullet fired, every private's pay, every widow's pension, every ship sunk or every hen-house wrecked by shell fire. In 1921 it concluded that Germany could and should pay £6,600,000,000 over the following thirty five years. At the time of the Treaty Germany also had to hand over most of her ocean-going merchant shipping to Britain.

3 Germany had to sign the Covenant of the League of Nations even though she was to be denied membership until she had proved that she had become a civilised and well-behaved nation.

land and 3.25 million in the new state of Czechoslovakia. Germans felt that self-determination had been applied to everybody but them and that these states had received land which was rightfully German. Germany alone had been forced to disarm, thus being left defenceless.

DEFENDERS OF THE TREATY

"By 1925 German steel production was twice that of Great Britain … Germany did very well in the fifteen years after 1919 despite its losses in that year and the later inflation and depression. The territorial settlement … was not in fact particularly severe. The return of Alsace-Lorraine to France was inevitable and only the Germans would have expected anything else; and the other cessions to Belgium … and Denmark were not crippling … The only standard of comparison by which the Versailles Treaty can be properly judged is that of the Germans' own treaty with the Russians at Brest-Litovsk … it deprived Russia of thirty four percent of her population, fifty four percent of her industrial undertakings and eighty nine percent of her coal mines. Nor was the cession of territory to the new Poland at all the tragedy the Germans insisted it was. … Poles had as much right to a national existence as the Germans. This the Germans never accepted … Nor was the loss of the German colonial empire a serious blow. It made far less difference to the Germans than the disappearance of their colonial empire would have made to the French; and the Germans would certainly have taken over the French colonies had the Allies been defeated."

(LCB Seaman, *Vienna to Versailles* pages 198–199)

PEACE AND FUTURE CANNON FODDER

Clemenceau: *"Strange I seem to hear a child crying."*

THE PEACE SETTLEMENT IN EASTERN EUROPE.

Compare Figure 9.1 showing Europe in 1920 with Figure 1.1 showing Europe in 1914. You will see that the peace settlement brought many new countries into being and that Russia and Austria-Hungary were much more affected by the peace than Germany.

Austria and Hungary became separate states. The old Austrian Empire was broken up. Those close slavonic cousins, the Czechs and the Slovaks, agreed to form Czechoslovakia. Croatia, Slovenia, and Bosnia joined Serbia in the new Kingdom of Yugoslavia. Poland reappeared for the first time since 1772, created with land from Germany, Russia and Austria. Finland, Estonia, Latvia and Lithuania emerged, blinking in the light of day, from Russian rule. Sadly, these countries quickly lapsed into dictatorship, persecuting their minority peoples in ways often worse than those they themselves had experienced under the Russians, Germans or Austrians. Only in Czechoslovakia did democracy survive until it was snuffed out by the invading Nazis in 1939.

Source A

A GERMAN REACTION TO VERSAILLES

Vengeance!
German nation!

Today in the Hall of Mirrors at Versailles a disgraceful treaty is being signed. Never forget it! On the spot where, in the glorious year of 1871, the German Empire in all its glory began, today German honour is dragged to the grave. Never forget it! The German people, with unceasing labour, will push forward to reconquer that place among the nations of the world to which they are entitled. There will be vengeance for the shame of 1919!

(From the right-wing, nationalist newspaper *Deutsche Zeitung* 28 June 1919. Published with a border of mourning black.)

Source B

ON WOODROW WILSON

"Woodrow Wilson's arrival in Paris on the morning of December 14 was, and probably still remains, the greatest triumphal progress which a human being has ever made. ... The crowds were so thick they were frightening. ... Placards hailing 'Wilson le juste' were posted everywhere. Weeping, shouting and crying 'Veelson!,' millions of Parisians fought for a better view of this saviour from the New World. ... Herbert Hoover observed, 'to them no such man of moral and political power and no such angel of peace had appeared on earth since Christ preached the Sermon on the Mount.' "
(Richard M Watt, *The Kings Depart*)

"Smuts and Botha ... regretted we had not one strong man who could last winter have secured a peace based on justice and Wilson's fourteen points. The latter mountebank they described as a man of empty words, who soars in a world of dreams and visions, regarding the mere execution of ideals and principles as beneath his intellect."
(Col. Richard Meinertzhagen, *Army Diary 1899–1926*)

Source C

THE PEACE TREATY

26 June 1919

"Dined with Smuts and Botha[1] ... They are loud in their denunciation of the Peace Treaty, which they says fosters the germs of new wars and that Germany is now compelled to throw herself into the hands of the Bolsheviks[2]. They say we had the most glorious opportunity to make a lasting and great peace, but instead we have frittered away our good name , our opportunities and our resources with nothing to show in return. They ascribe our total failure in Paris to a weak-kneed policy of pandering to the Latin races[3] ...

Perhaps I should add my own humble view. The Germans are the most civilised, the most progressive, the most intelligent and the most aggressive of European peoples. To keep them down perpetually is a hopeless and dangerous task ... I therefore regard the Treaty as dangerously repressive. The German peoples ... will react violently to what they regard as grossly unjust. They will clutch at any straw which offers them hope—perhaps to Russia and Communism—or to some violent little revolutionary of their own who offers them hope and revenge; the Germans cannot remain under-dogs ... this wretched Treaty will make them long for revenge. There is too much French spite and hatred in the Treaty and too much American dreaming."

(Col. Richard Meinertzhagen, *Army Diary 1899-1926*
Meinertzhagen was a staff officer in the British Army.)

[1] Smuts and Botha = South African Afrikaner generals
[2] Bolsheviks. The name given to the Russian Communist Party who seized power in 1917.
[3] Latin races: These include the French and Italians.

The League of Nations

PEACEKEEPING 1919 TO 1930

In January 1918, while Germany still appeared to have a chance of winning the war, the American President, Woodrow Wilson, issued his fourteen points for peace. (See page 73.) In the points, Wilson outlined ideas and changes for keeping the peace and preventing another world war. Among these ideas was the setting up of a League of Nations.

He said, "… it is our duty to … see to it that the mothers of America and the mothers of France and England and Italy and Belgium and all those other suffering nations should never be called on to make this sacrifice again. The great thing that these men left us is … the League of Nations."

The idea behind the League was simple. All the leading democratic countries would be members. If any country attacked another then the countries of the League would act together against the aggressor and force it to stop.

The League was set up at the Versailles Conference. The details of how it was to be run and how it was to work were described in its Covenant, the League rule book. The defeated countries all had to agree that they would abide by the Covenant when they signed their peace treaties. At first defeated countries like Germany, Austria, Hungary and Turkey were not allowed to join, nor was Russia which had become communist.

ORGANISATION OF THE LEAGUE

The League had its headquarters at Geneva in neutral Switzerland. Its Assembly met at these headquarters. The Assembly was the League's parliament in which all member nations had one vote. It debated important issues and decided on the general policy of the League. It also controlled the budget and decided which countries were fit to become members. Unlike the parliaments of its member countries, it was not in permanent session.

The Council of the League made decisions on the day-to-day running of the League. In 1930 it had five permanent members: Britain, France, Italy,

OVERWEIGHTED

PRESIDENT WILSON: "Here's your olive branch. Now get busy."
Dove of Peace: "Of course I want to please everybody: but isn't this a bit thick."

Japan and Germany. The USA never joined and Germany was only allowed membership in 1926. The Council always contained a number of temporary members chosen by the Assembly. It also met in Geneva.

The Secretariat was a body of permanent officials who kept records and recorded the decisions made by the Assembly and by the Council.

The Permanent Court of Justice was based in the Hague in Holland. It was made up of distinguished judges from member nations. It could settle legal disputes between nations or give advice to the Assembly or Council on matters to do with International law.

The Covenant of the League described a logical system of measures which could be used to control an aggressor nation. A hierarchy of punishments, or sanctions, was available.

Step 1—Moral Sanctions
A country which violated the rights of another could be rebuked by the League, warned about its behaviour and told to stop. In effect this amounted to a good telling off.

Step 2—Economic Sanctions
In more serious cases, or if a country did not respond to moral sanctions, economic sanctions could be applied. Member nations would be told to stop trading with the aggressor. They would sell nothing to her, buy nothing from her and lend no money to her. This could ruin businesses in the country concerned and force it to do as it was told.

Step 3—Military Sanctions
In the most serious cases the League could call on its members to provide military, naval or air forces for armed action against the culprit. Aggressors could also be expelled from the League.

HOW STRONG WAS THE LEAGUE?
The idea of the League was very popular with ordinary people in Europe who were anxious to avoid another war. It was less popular with their governments.

Although its President, Woodrow Wilson, had been the driving force behind the League, the USA refused to join. American presidents can sign treaties but Congress, the US parliament, and most of the State Legislatures (parliaments) also have to ratify, or vote for, those treaties. Wilson could not persuade the rest of the USA to accept the League and she never joined. Many Americans feared that they might be dragged into another European war which really had very little to do with America.

By 1919 the USA was the world's richest and strongest country and unlike the countries of Europe, she was not exhausted by war. The failure of the USA to join the League which her President had started left the League seriously weakened. None of the governments in Europe felt as strongly about the League as Wilson had. It could be claimed that they never really tried to make it work.

DID THE LEAGUE HAVE ANY SUCCESSES?
Humanitarian Work
In the years after the war the League did a great deal of useful humanitarian work. Fridtjof Nansen, a Norwegian arctic explorer, became the League's Commissioner for refugees. He helped 400,000 refugees, displaced by the war, to return home or to find new homes. The League also did valuable work against the slave trade in Africa and tried to control the drug trade.

Settling Disputes
The League did manage to settle some disputes, but these were all between small states which could be leaned upon or between states which were willing to cooperate with the League. For instance, Finland and Sweden both claimed the Aaland Islands, which lay in the Baltic Sea, between the two countries. Sweden was keen to see the League succeed and accepted its verdict when the islands were awarded to Finland.

DID THE LEAGUE FAIL BADLY IN THE 1920s?
A number of disputes took place which involved middle-sized to large countries. Here the League either failed to act or allowed another body to act on its behalf.

The Ruhr 1923
By 1923 Germany was a little behind with her reparation payments. The French and the Belgians sent their armies into her most important industrial area, the Ruhr, in order to enforce payment. Germany seemed to be the victim of aggression and Sweden was going to raise it with the League. The French said that they would leave the League if this happened so the Swedes and the League did nothing. The French finally withdrew after the German economy had collapsed and they had forced the Germans to promise to start paying reparations once more. A bad example had been set.

Corfu 1923

In 1923 the Italians, under Mussolini, seized the Greek island of Corfu. They blamed the Greeks for the death of an Italian general who had been involved in surveying the border between Greece and Albania. There was little evidence that the Greeks were to blame. Mussolini ignored a request from the League to withdraw from Corfu. At this point the Conference of Ambassadors took over from the League. This body consisted of representatives of the countries who had been involved with the Versailles Treaty. They ordered the Greeks to pay compensation and Mussolini withdrew. The victim had been punished! The fact that the League could be so easily brushed aside when a major power was the aggressor was a bad sign. It was obvious that the League would not take on a powerful nation simply to get justice for a small one.

The Disarmament Conference

Many people believed that the arms race before the First World War had been a major cause of the war. The League set itself the task of persuading the nations of the world to cut down on their arms and armed forces in order to preserve peace. It was decided to hold a disarmament conference in Geneva.

Although all nations agreed, in theory, that disarmament was a good thing they could not agree, in practice, how this was to be done. The League took twelve years to organise a conference with an agenda which the nations were willing to discuss. The conference met in 1932 but the delegates could agree on very little. The French rejected German demands that they disarm to German levels. In 1933 Hitler withdrew Germany from the conference and also from the League.

HOPEFUL SIGNS

For a while in the mid-'20s there were hopeful signs that Europe might manage to remain at peace. The French Foreign Minister, Aristide Briand, and the German Foreign Minister, Gustav Stresemann, both wanted their countries to get on well with each other.

In 1924 the Dawes plan was brought in giving Germany longer to pay off her reparations and in 1925 the Locarno Agreement was signed in which Germany accepted as final her borders with France and Belgium.

In 1928 Briand and the American Secretary of State, Frank B Kellogg drew up the Kellogg-Briand pact which sixty two nations signed, promising never to go to war, except in self-defence.

WAS THE LEAGUE MORE SUCCESSFUL IN THE 1930s?

In fact, in the 1930s things got worse—much worse. Even before the unsuccessful disarmament conference, Japan had seized the Chinese province of Manchuria (1931). She refused to obey the League and left the League in 1933.

In 1929 the Great Depression began in America. Soon millions of people were out of work in every country of the world. The desperation which this caused brought Adolf Hitler to power in Germany.

Italy attacked and conquered Abyssinia (Ethiopia) in 1935 and, when condemned by the League, left it as Japan had done earlier.

The League's inability to control the aggression of these militaristic states (Germany, Japan and Italy) led to the Second World War.

Source

THE LEAGUE OF NATIONS:

The League of Nations … is not a mere expression … of the necessity for international friendship and a good understanding. It provides the machinery by which practical effect might be given to these principles.

Should disputes unhappily arise, the disputants will find themselves in an assembly of impartial and unbiased councillors, whose sole aim will be to remove misunderstandings …

(Lord Curzon, a British politician, quoted in the *League of Nations Official Journal* in February 1920)